THE SIERRAS OF EXTREMADURA

About the Author

Gisela Radant Wood is a walker, writer, photographer, avid reader and passionate about Extremadura. She has lived in the Sierra de Montánchez for the past 10 years and walks there on a regular basis. Home is a finca outside the village of Almoharín with a husband, a dog, seven sheep, occasional lambs, four hens and 150 olive trees. Ten years ago Gisela set up the website www.walkingextremadura.com and is actively involved in promoting the area as a walking paradise. This is her second book about walking in Extremadura.

Gisela loves the social side of walking with friends in the Almoharín walking group, but really prefers the quiet of walking alone in the countryside she loves.

THE SIERRAS OF EXTREMADURA

by Gisela Radant Wood

JUNIPER HOUSE, MURLEY MOSS,
OXENHOLME ROAD, KENDAL, CUMBRIA LA9 7RL
www.cicerone.co.uk

First edition 2017
ISBN: 978 1 85284 848 4

Printed by KHL Printing, Singapore
A catalogue record for this book is available from the British Library.

Route mapping by Lovell Johns www.lovelljohns.com
Contains OpenStreetMap.org data © OpenStreetMap
contributors, CC-BY-SA. NASA relief data courtesy of ESRI

All photographs are by the author unless otherwise stated.

Updates to this Guide

While every effort is made by our authors to ensure the accuracy of guidebooks as they go to print, changes can occur during the lifetime of an edition. Any updates that we know of for this guide will be on the Cicerone website (www.cicerone.co.uk/848/updates), so please check before planning your trip. We also advise that you check information about such things as transport, accommodation and shops locally. Even rights of way can be altered over time.

The route maps in this guide are derived from publicly-available data, databases and crowd-sourced data. As such they have not been through the detailed checking procedures that would generally be applied to a published map from an official mapping agency, although naturally we have reviewed them closely in the light of local knowledge as part of the preparation of this guide.

We are always grateful for information about any discrepancies between a guidebook and the facts on the ground, sent by email to updates@cicerone.co.uk or by post to Cicerone, Juniper House, Murley Moss, Oxenholme Road, Kendal LA9 7RL, United Kingdom.

Register your book: To sign up to receive free updates, special offers and GPX files where available, register your book at www.cicerone.co.uk.

Front cover: Trevejo Castle dominates the small village of Trevejo in the western Sierra de Gata

CONTENTS

Symbols used on route maps

~~	route
---	alternative route
Ⓢ	start point
Ⓕ	finish point
ⓈⒻ	start/finish point
	woodland
	urban areas
	international border
	regional border
▲	summit
⬆	refuge
■	building
♰ ♰ †	monastery/convent/cross
🏰	castle
•	water feature
≶	waterfall
✳	viewpoint
⁙	mirador
≍	bridge
戸	picnic area
≡	cattle grid
🚌	bus stop
•	other feature

Relief
in metres

2400–2600
2200–2400
2000–2200
1800–2000
1600–1800
1400–1600
1200–1400
1000–1200
800–1000
600–800
400–600
200–400
0–200

SCALE: 1:50,000

0 kilometres 0.5   1
0 miles   0.5

Contour lines are
drawn at 25m intervals
and highlighted at
100m intervals.

GPX files

GPX files for all routes can be downloaded free at www.cicerone.co.uk/848/GPX.

Waterfall in the Sierra de Gredos

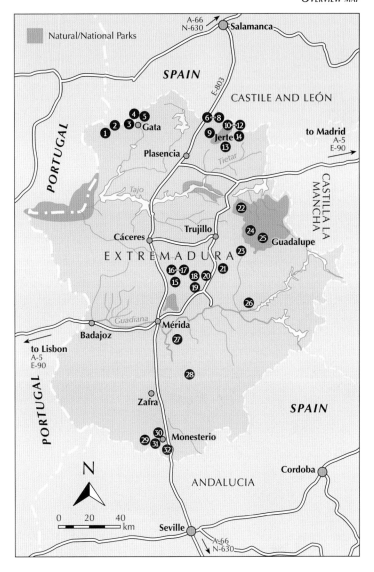

Natural/National Parks

SPAIN

CASTILE AND LEÓN

PORTUGAL

Salamanca

to Madrid
A-5
E-90

Gata

Plasencia

Jerte

Tiétar

CASTILLA LA MANCHA

Tajo

Trujillo

Guadalupe

Cáceres

E X T R E M A D U R A

Guadiana

Mérida

Badajoz

to Lisbon
A-5
E-90

PORTUGAL

Zafra

SPAIN

Monesterio

Córdoba

N

ANDALUCIA

0   20   40
km

Seville

A-66
N-630

Chozo (traditional shepherd's hut) in the Sierra de Gredos (Walk 14)

INTRODUCTION

Walking down to Puente Sacristán (Walk 10)

Ancient footpaths lined with yellow broom, purple lavender and white cistus lead in and out of dark pine woods that provide cool shade. High rolling pastures, bright with wildflowers, are framed by snow-capped mountains which puncture the blue sky. The white-washed, red-roofed buildings of small villages can be seen tucked into the folds of hillsides. Cows graze the lower slopes and the valley floor, their bells providing the only intermittent sound; griffon vultures circle above the peaks. There is not another person in sight.

Extremadura remains Spain's least-known and least-visited region, but very gradually, walkers, lovers of nature's beauty and seekers of peace

are finding their way there. Many arrive not knowing quite what to expect. None leave disappointed.

The region is sparsely populated in modern terms: it has only 26 residents per square kilometre, while England has 406. The largest city in Extremadura is Badajoz with a little over 150,000 inhabitants. Most people live in small towns or villages each with their distinct character and quite separate from the next. Ribbon development does not exist in Extremadura.

What does exist, in abundance, is open countryside, mountains, hills, valleys, lakes, rivers, forests, pasture and thousands of kilometres of paths criss-crossing the region. These paths are perfect for walking: some are part

11

A chance meeting in the Sierra de Gredos in June

of an ancient communication network from the days when people walked everywhere; some are delightful meanderings around the agricultural areas that surround every village. The oldest are paved with granite, others are soft earth. Many are shaded with trees and have verges profuse with flowers, in season.

The untouched countryside is a haven for wildlife and birds, and Extremadura has many protected areas. Monfragüe National Park lies at the heart of where the Tiétar and Tajo rivers meet; the area is covered in forest and is famous as a nesting site for many species of raptor. Further west, where the Tajo crosses into Portugal, the Tajo International Natural Park has been established where the rivers Erjas and Sever join the bigger river. The oldest rocks in the peninsula sit in the middle of the Cáceres plain, and the Monumental Park of Los Barruecos has spectacular granite rocks of at least 575 million years old. Its lakes attract birds year-round.

Cornalvo Natural Park is, in reality, a huge area of *dehesa* – open parkland covered with spaced-out evergreen holm oaks. Its lake, formed by a dam built in Roman times, attracts birds and wildfowl year-round. La Garganta de los Infiernos Natural Park in the Jerte valley incorporates part of the southern slopes of the Sierra de Gredos, while as recently as 2011 a GeoPark was formed uniting the areas of Las Villuercas, Los Ibores and Jara.

All of these parks have hundreds of kilometres of designated and signed walking paths and are testimony to Extremadura's continuing commitment to preserving its natural environment.

The biggest Protection Areas are, without doubt, for birds. These have the acronym ZEPA (Zona Especial de Protección para Aves); the Sierra de Pela and the Sierra Grande de Hornachos, both featured in this book, are ZEPA areas. The Sierra de San Pedro and much of the area around Cáceres are also designated ZEPA.

Quite apart from its natural heritage, Extremadura also boasts three World Heritage Sites: Roman Mérida, Renaissance Cáceres and Guadalupe. These cities, along with Trujillo, Coria, Plasencia, Badajoz and Jerez de los Caballeros, to name but a few, are wonderful places to explore on foot and soak up the atmosphere of past centuries. However, Cáceres, Mérida and Badajoz also have their dynamic, modern sides, which can add a different dimension to a walking holiday.

GEOGRAPHY AND GEOLOGY

Extremadura sits west of Madrid and east of the Portuguese border. It is the fifth largest autonomous region in Spain and is divided into two provinces: Cáceres and Badajoz. At 41,633 square kilometres it is just larger than Switzerland. From the border with Castile and León in the north to the Andalucian border in the south is 280 kilometres. On a map the region looks like a layered cake: from

Granite boulders are a feature of almost every walk in the northern and central sierras

north to south are the Sistema Central mountains, the Tajo river basin, the Montes de Toledo, the Guadiana river basin and the Sierra Morena.

Across the north, within the Sistema Central, lie the Sierra de Gata, Sierra de Béjar and the Sierra de Gredos. These forested sierras contain the highest peaks in Extremadura, reaching over 2000m. They are snow-covered for up to six months of the year. Springs that well up high in the sierras are engorged with snow melt and form numerous rivers which keep the valleys permanently green.

South of these mountains lies the Tajo river basin with its main tributaries: the Tiétar, Alagón, Almonte and Ibor. The Tajo is the longest river in the Iberian peninsula.

Strung across the middle of Extremadura are the Montes de Toledo with numerous smaller granite sierras. Some, such as the Sierra de San Pedro in the west, are low hills rather than mountains, but the Sierra de Montánchez reaches a respectable 994m.

The mountains in the Sierra de las Villuercas are not granite; their geological structure is mainly composed of slates and quartzites and the walking experience is very different there. The sierras run parallel to each other, largely ruling out circular walks. The Almonte and Ibor rivers, which flow north to feed the Tajo, rise in Las Villuercas while the Ruecas and Guadalupe rivers are tributaries of the Guadiana river to the south.

The Jaranda Valley near Guijo (Walk 14)

Griffon vultures can be seen from many of the walks in this book

The Guadiana is also fed by the Zújar and Matachel tributaries and forms part of the border between the two provinces. As it flows west and turns south it becomes the border with Portugal. The river feeds the Orellana canal system, which irrigates thousands of hectares of agricultural land producing maize, rice and tomatoes among other crops.

The Sierra Morena, with peaks over 1000m, lies to the south and straddles the border between Extremadura and Andalucia. The sierra is made up of granite and quartzite, as well as softer materials such as slate and gneiss. While on average 1000m lower than the peaks in the Sistema Central, the Sierra Morena is nevertheless an important mountain range within the overall geography of Spain. It provides the watershed for two of the peninsula's five major rivers: the Guadiana to the north of the sierra and the Guadalquivar to the south.

ANIMALS AND BIRDS

The wildlife in Extremadura is still genuinely wild. Depending on the habitat and the time of the year that you visit, red deer, wild boar, rabbit, Iberian hare, fox, badger, wild cat, pine marten, genet, otter and mongoose may be seen. Lynx are much rarer.

Extremadura has long been known by birdwatchers as a very special place. It is on many migratory routes, with diverse species stopping off in summer or winter. Cranes feed

15

in their thousands in wetlands. Storks make nests on every available high spot on churches and castles alike. The mountains provide habitats for many species of vulture, eagle, harrier, buzzard, kite and hawk. The forests house pigeons, doves and woodpeckers – very often heard but not seen. The river valleys are home to the heron, stork, lapwing, grebe, ducks and any number of smaller water-loving birds. The open expanses provide homes to great bustards, especially in La Serena in the south-east of Extremadura. The general countryside is full of azure-winged magpie, colourful bee-eater, flashy hoopoe, crested lark, shrike, golden oriole, dove, owl and many small songbirds.

FLOWERS AND PLANTS

Extremadura's natural habitats support an enormous diversity of flowers, flowering bushes, trees and vegetation. In spring it is impossible to do many of the walks in this book without stepping on carpets of colour created by thousands of wildflowers: Barbary nut, Spanish iris, field gladiolus, foxglove, asphodel, birdsfoot trefoil, snake's-head fritillary, lupin, yellow and white daisy, vetch and orchid. The distinctive purple that covers the dehesa in April and May is courtesy of viper's bugloss.

Poor soil and stony sierra slopes are no barrier to tough but beautiful bushes: white and pink flowering cistus, white and yellow broom, retama, lavender, Mediterranean Daphne,

Clockwise from left: Cystus Albidus; Aricia Agestis on a Leontodon Hispidus; lichen on granite boulder; sawfly orchid (Ophrys Tenthredinifera)

Spanish heath, rosemary, juniper and tansy. They form a backdrop to the walks in spring and early summer.

Agriculture has provided numerous trees that add their own colourful blossoms in spring: olive, cherry, orange and almond trees have been cultivated for over a millennium. The sight of the Jerte valley in spring, covered in cherry blossom as far as the eye can see, is unforgettable. The leaves of the fig trees of Almoharín give shade in the summer, and in the winter their bare branches add a sculptural structure to the countryside.

Within the huge forests are the indigenous oaks – holm, cork and Pyrenean. Spanish chestnut, terebinth, alder and a variety of pine underpin the diversity of trees so important to the ecology of the area.

Rock painting, Sierra de Peñas Blancas (Walk 27)

HUMAN HISTORY

During the long Stone Age, small clans of hunter-gatherers arrived in the Iberian Peninsula, as evidenced by cave paintings in the region. By the Bronze Age, settlements of livestock herders, agriculturalists and harvesters were established. In the Iron Age separate societies emerged.

The Phoenicians were the first traders to reach up the rivers into the area that would become Extremadura. They were followed by the Greeks, whose main trading partners were the Celtiberians, a group of distinct and merged tribes of Iberians and Celts. They had arrived, possibly from Gaul, in sporadic waves between 3000 and 700BC. The Lusitani, who settled on both sides of the River Tajo, and the Vettones, their allies, who settled in the Alagón valley, along with the Turduli/Turdetani were the principal tribes occupying Extremadura. The countryside is littered with the reminders of their tradition of building dolmens to bury their dead.

The Carthaginians followed the Phoenicians around 575BC. They were originally happy just to trade, but after they lost the First Punic War to Rome (264–241BC) they established a small military presence to salvage their pride. The Lusitani and the Vettones were not about to let that happen: for over 30 years they resisted the Carthaginians in a sustained guerrilla war.

Horses are still a part of everyday life for many local people

The Romans came to Iberia to fight their enemy the Carthaginians. After defeating them the Romans looked around at the wealth of the region – mainly in agriculture but also in metals and marble – and they stayed. They established camps, built defensive forts and intermarried with the local population. The capital of Lusitania, their westernmost province, was established at Ermita Augusta, today's Mérida. After the Roman Empire fell, the Visigoths held sway from early AD400 to 711 when the first of many invasions by Arab and Berber tribes, collectively known as the Moors, started. It took the Visigoths, mixed with peoples from the north of Spain and reinvented as the Christians, 500 years to reconquer Extremadura.

In the 1500s, Extremadura provided the majority of *conquistadores* for the plundering of the New World. Trujillo and Cáceres still display the results of some of the wealth brought back, but most of the treasure went to fighting interminable religious wars. Extremadura gradually slid into obscurity; the landlords lived as landlords do while the people worked the land in abject poverty.

The Peninsula Wars of the early 19th century ravaged the land. The forces of Spain, Portugal and the British on the one hand, and Napoleonic France on the other, pillaged their way through the region. The 20th century brought no respite: the civil war saw defeat for republican-minded people. Dictator Franco took his revenge in neglect of the area for decades. Many people sought work in other European countries; people over 60 may not speak English but very often have enough Dutch or German to pass a pleasant time of day with visitors from those countries.

Today, modern roads and investment in agriculture and tourism have brought a new dynamic to the region. The people of Extremadura are genuinely open and friendly. They are fiercely proud of their home villages but are well aware of what is going on in the wider world. However, the care of the family, the village, the countryside, the traditional way of life: this is what matters to modern local people.

There is a growing realisation that the region's centuries of isolation have handed down a precious heritage. Enormous tracts of Extremadura are still untouched. Active conservation has, so far, kept at bay 21st-century manias such as unsightly and noisy wind farms. Power demand is met with solar panel farms, which are silent, less intrusive and allow the sheep to graze the land as they have done for centuries. The future of Extremadura looks good. Long may its beauty be enjoyed while also being protected.

GETTING THERE

By air
Extremadura has no international airport. Most visitors fly to Madrid, Lisbon or Seville and hire a car. Hire cars are available from the big car rental companies at all three airports, or visitors who prefer not to drive from an airport city can take the train or bus to Extremadura (see below) and hire a car locally. See Appendix D for car hire contact details.

To Madrid
Madrid's airport – called Adolfo Suárez Madrid-Barajas – is perhaps the obvious choice as it has the most direct daily flights connected with the most destinations. BA-Iberia (www.britishairways.com) connect to almost everywhere in the world and are competitive in their pricing with off-peak bargains. However, not all regional airports have a direct flight; many have connections in London's Heathrow or Gatwick airports.

Madrid is well served by several low-cost airlines: both Easyet (www.easyjet.com) and Ryanair (www.ryanair.com) offer flights from all the major airports in Europe, and some regional airports have limited flights. Vueling (www.vueling.com) and Norwegian (www.norwegian.com) are both low-cost airlines gaining in popularity. Vueling tends to fly with a stopover in Barcelona, its hub. Both Vueling and Norwegian run limited flights in the winter months.

Lufthansa (www.lufthansa.com) and KLM (www.klm.com) are medium-priced airlines that fly to Madrid from a staggering number of places, although some have connections and stopovers at other airports.

To Lisbon

Lisbon is well served by all the above-listed airlines, as well as Portugal's own airline, Tap Portugal (www.flytap.com).

To Seville

Seville is the least well served airport. BA-Iberia operate there with daily direct flights from London Gatwick, but flights from Amsterdam or Berlin, for example, are via Heathrow or Gatwick. Easyjet also fly direct to Seville daily from Gatwick. Ryanair provide a daily flight from London Stanstead and Brussels, while Dublin fares less well with three flights a week.

All information is correct at the time of writing (2017) but it is vital to do your own research.

By rail

Trains from Europe arrive in Madrid at Chamartín Station. From there, take the Metro (subway) to Atocha Renfe, look for the Cercanías platforms and take a Cáceres–Mérida–Badajoz train. Get off at Navalmoral de la Mata or Plasencia for the northern sierras;

Cáceres for the central sierras; Mérida for the southern sierras. See bus and car hire information to get from these towns to the walks.

There were no direct trains from Lisbon that stop in Extremadura at the time of writing (2017). Trains from Seville go to Mérida, Cáceres and beyond but need connections. For more information see www.renfe.com.

By bus

Buses run from Madrid's Estación Sur. The Metro stop is Mendez Alvaro. A number of bus companies go to different parts of Extremadura. Avanzabus (www.avanzabus.com) run a service from Lisbon but with limited stops in Extremadura; there is a good bus service from Seville. For useful websites see Appendix D.

By car

Drivers entering Spain from the north should head for Burgos, Valladolid and Salamanca and pick up the N-630 Ruta de la Plata or the E-803/A-66 motorway (they run side-by-side but are not the same). Extremadura is reached through the Puerto de Béjar,

DISTANCES TO EXTREMADURA TOWNS FROM MAJOR AIRPORTS	
Madrid to Gata – 330km	Lisbon to Guadalupe – 410km
Madrid to Jerte – 235km	Lisbon to Monesterio – 355km
Madrid to Guadalupe – 260km	Seville to Gata – 375km
Madrid to Monesterio – 460km	Seville to Jerte – 380km
Lisbon to Gata – 330km	Seville to Guadalupe – 325km
Lisbon to Jerte – 424km	Seville to Monesterio – 98km

where it is possible to stop and enjoy some walking in the Ambroz valley or continue on to the chosen destination.

Driving in Extremadura is a real pleasure as there are so few vehicles on the roads in comparison to almost every other European country. It has some of the best-kept motorways in Europe but they are usually only two-lane. Smaller roads are well kept but village streets are generally tiny and confusing. The Guardia Civil make regular checks on vehicles at round-abouts so make sure yours is roadwor-thy and that your licence and ID are in order to avoid the on-the-spot fines.

Local driving habits are civilized and mainly polite, although the tradi-tion on roundabouts of keeping to the lane on the right, no matter whether turning left or not, is confusing at first.

The roads around villages tend to have slow-moving tractors and trailers during December and January for the olive harvest, during June and July for the tomatoes and fruits and August for the figs. Be patient.

By ferry

Brittany Ferries (www.brittany-ferries. co.uk) sail from Portsmouth to Bilbao and from Plymouth to Santander. Once there, head for Burgos, Valladolid, Salamanca and follow the Ruta de la Plata down into Extremadura. From Bilbao to Hervás in the Ambroz Valley is 500km and from Santander to Hervás it is 470km. Add an extra 285km to drive down to Monesterio.

If you want to bring your own vehicle and tour Extremadura it is a good way of travelling to the area.

Folk music is an important part of any local fiesta

GETTING AROUND

The most practical way to get around Extremadura is by car. The network of motorways and main roads in Extremadura is excellent. Minor roads linking small villages are generally good and the drives can be very scenic.

The rail company Renfe (www.renfe.com) runs trains that link all the main cities across Extremadura, and main railways stations have bus connections. Spanish trains usually run on time and every ticket holder has a seat. Train fares are reasonable – 300km between Madrid and Cáceres is around €40, with discounts for young people and students. Over 60s can buy a *Trajeta Dorada* (Golden Card) for €5 at any railway station by showing their passport or proof of age. This card allows immediate discounts on all rail travel. (Prices correct in 2017.)

Plasencia, Cáceres, Trujillo, Mérida and Badajoz all have main bus stations. Even the smallest villages from which walks start and finish have bus stops, although services may often be limited to one bus per day in each direction. Note that services can be disrupted at any time and on public and local holidays they do not run at all. Getting around by bus is in theory a good idea but in practice may be complicated.

See Appendix D for contact details of local transport providers.

WHEN TO GO

March in the Sierra de Gredos

March and April are normally warm and sunny with occasional showers, and are lovely months for wildflowers and nesting bird activity. May and June still have flowers but can be hot and dry, while July and August are very hot and walking is only possible early or late in the day – preferably by a river or under shady trees in the northern sierras. Things have cooled down by September and October but the countryside stays dry until the rains come – generally October/November. All of Extremadura can be enjoyed in November and December: they are glorious months with the forested slopes of the sierras ablaze with autumn colour. There may be rain but not usually for days on end, and migrating birds visit the region at this time. January and February can be cold with showers, but flowers start to bloom along with the almond blossom. Snow is not usual in the central and southern sierras, but in the north the sierras can be freezing with substantial falls of snow.

Always check the weather before setting out – try www.eltiempo.es (search for villages individually to get local forecasts).

BASES AND ACCOMMODATION

Bases
Extremadura is vast. The walks in this book are grouped around central places to stay, which should aid planning and, in some cases, make daily transport arrangements unnecessary.

There are tourist information offices in most of the towns, and places that do not have a dedicated tourist office usually provide tourist information at the town hall. See Appendix D for contact details.

Northern sierras
In the Sierra de Gata, San Martín de Trevejo, Gata and Robledillo de Gata are charming old villages with historical character, pleasant squares, places to eat and a few shops. They all offer a good choice of accommodation.

The small village of La Garganta offers no accommodation but Baños de Montemayor and Hervás, both within easy distance of La Garganta, are thriving tourist centres with excellent facilities including banks, cash machines, shops, restaurants and tourist offices.

La Garganta

Jerte is a popular and busy tourist town with good facilities and accommodation options to suit all pockets. It is especially pretty – and busy – at cherry blossom time of the year (April/May) so book early. Jarandilla de la Vera is also an excellent tourist centre with a variety of accommodation, including the 15th-century Parador de Jarandilla de la Vera. The tourist office has plenty of information on local routes for walkers.

Central sierras
Montánchez and Almoharín are small towns with banks, shops, cafés, bars and restaurants. They offer a quality choice of village and rural accommodation. There is no tourist office that covers the area, in spite of advertising that there is, but the local town halls are helpful, especially in Almoharín where English is spoken.

Guadalupe is an international tourist centre. It has a *hospedería* and a *parador* as well as numerous hotels and *casas rurales* (see 'Types of accommodation', below). The tourist office is very good and well stocked with information leaflets and maps of local walks.

Southern sierras
Alange, La Zarza and Hornachos are good places to stay with a full range of facilities and accommodation choices. Mérida, the capital of Extremadura, is also not far from these towns. The tourist offices, especially in Mérida, are useful places to visit.

Monesterio is an excellent base for walking and offers a variety of accommodation. The tourist office, run by Enrique, where English is spoken, is sited in the Jamón Museum which is certainly worth a visit.

Types of accommodation
Hospederías are usually situated near an area of tourist interest but could also be found within quite a large town. They are government-owned and -run hotels of good quality and facilities at a medium price range: around €75–€125 per couple per night including breakfast. They can be modern buildings or well-converted old properties.

Paradors are also government-owned and -run but are definitely in old historic buildings such as convents, monasteries and castles. They are usually situated in older parts of historical towns. They are sympathetically converted but retain many original features to give an atmosphere of comfort but within a slice of history. The price range in Extremadura is between €150–€230 per couple per night including breakfast.

Casas rurales can be almost anything from a grand estate farmhouse to a modern house but are usually situated in the countryside or in a small rural village. They are graded with oak tree symbols – one is basic, two is medium and three is superior. Casas rurales can be rented in different ways:

- rent the entire building and be completely self-sufficient
- rent the whole building but breakfast is provided and rooms are cleaned
- rent a room and share the kitchen and other common rooms with other people (whom you will not know) who are also just renting rooms
- rent a room but the owners live in the building and provide breakfast and clean the rooms.

Prices vary from around €35 per person or €50 per couple per night, including breakfast, up to over €100 for luxurious and well-facilitated places. It is important to research casas rurales carefully but many are fabulous places in beautiful locations.

Many hospederías and paradors offer reduced prices mid-week,

Tuesday to Thursday. Some of the offers can be half-price so it is worth doing some careful planning in advance.

Recommendations for accommodation throughout Extremadura can be found at www.walkingextremadura.com/where-to-stay.html.

FOOD AND DRINK

Extremaduran (*Extremeño*) food is delicious and healthy. It is a region whose biggest economy – and export – is agriculture. Not to be missed are *jamón* (ham) from Montánchez and Monesterio; *Torta de Casar* sheep cheese; figs (especially the chocolate variety) from Almoharín; cherries from the Jerte valley; raspberries from La Vera; jams from Guijo de Santa Bárbara; and red wines from Badajoz

Black pigs at Monesterio (Walk 30)

The best tapas are often found in village bars

province – especially Monasterio de Tentudía in the blue bottle.

November is the time for mushrooms and many towns do mushroom tapas trails. During the winter months, local hunters provide restaurants with game for their huge stews of venison, wild boar, rabbit, partridge and other game birds – delicious, organic and fresh.

Try to avoid the tourist plazas in the large cities and opt, instead, for the places the locals eat. Most small villages will have a bar that offers food, even if it is only tapas. Others offer *raciones* – intended to be smaller than a meal but often just as huge. Bear in mind that bars may keep vague hours.

Local cafés and bars open early; 6.00 am is not unusual. They serve coffee and breakfasts, which can be anything from *churros* (doughnut pastry sticks), to *tostadas*, with cheese and ham or the traditional olive oil and tomato paste.

Village shops close on Saturday at noon and do not reopen until Monday at 10am. They will stay closed on public holidays and *puentes* – days that bridge holidays and weekends.

LANGUAGE

Castilian Spanish is the language used in Extremadura, although you may well wonder if this is really the case when you're in conversation with a local. The Extremeño dialect is difficult to follow and the 's' at the end of many words disappears altogether. However, the people are friendly and patient and will wait happily while you try out your Spanish – although their answer may not be so slow. The words *habla despacio* ('speak slowly') are handy. Many people involved in tourism do speak some English, though.

MONEY

Spain's currency is the Euro. Avoid high denomination notes when paying cash in village shops and bars. Credit and bank cards can be used in towns in major supermarket chains. Paradors and hospederías will accept card payment for accommodation but some casas rurales may want cash. ATMs are widespread but not in every small village, so plan ahead.

COMMUNICATIONS

As a general principle, the bigger the town, the better the communications. Smaller villages nearly all have one public phone box and a post office (the latter often only open from 8.30am to 9.30am, Monday to Friday). Mobile phone coverage is widespread but this can fluctuate in mountainous regions – although in the author's experience all the walks in this book seem to be covered. Internet coverage is available in most hotels and casas rurales, but if a daily connection is important to you, check before making a booking.

WHAT TO TAKE ON A WALK

Everyone has favourite bits of kit they like to take on a walk, but a few items are common for an enjoyable – and safe – walking experience:

- map, compass, GPS device, mobile phone, torch, knife
- basic first aid kit; plasters, antiseptic cream, bandage
- mosquito and insect repellent
- camera, binoculars
- hat, sunscreen and sunglasses (useful all year round)
- waterproofs
- appropriate footwear: should be able to cope with a mixture of terrains – granite can be slippery when wet and harder soles are not a good idea.
- comfortable clothing made of natural fibres
- walking poles (optional)
- water: essential year-round – at least 1L per person
- high-energy snacks: chocolate or dried fruits

WAYMARKING

Of the waymarking you're likely to encounter on walks in this guide, 'GR' refers to *Gran Recorrido*, a long-distance footpath with numbered stages and white and red waymarks; 'PR' refers to *Pequeño Recorrido*, a short-distance footpath that is numbered and signed in white and yellow; and local routes are indicated by the letters 'SL', *Sendero Local*, with white and green waymarks.

Signage comes in many forms in Extremadura

Important routes may have their own fingerposts at junctions. Some routes have helpful hand-painted signs and arrows on walls or gates, while others simply have cairns – which are excellent indicators, especially on higher, wilder sierras.

In recent years there has been a huge improvement in waymarking, but many routes remain patchy or unsigned.

MAPS

The maps provided in this book should be all that you need to complete each walk. However, the relevant Instituto Geográfica Nacional (IGN) map is listed in the information given at the start of the walk. Maps can be purchased directly from IGN, or from other retailers such as Stanfords. See Appendix D for contact details.

The following maps are useful for the walks in this book:
- IGN 573 Gata 1:50,000
- IGN 576 Cabezuela del Valle 1:50,000
- IGN 681 Castañar de Ibor 1:50,000
- IGN 706 Madroñera 1:50,000
- IGN 707 Logrosán 1:50,000
- IGN 730 Montánchez 1:50,000
- IGN 803 Almendralejo 1:50,000
- IGN 897 Monesterio 1:50,000
- IGN 573-111 Eljas 1:25,000
- IGN 599-II Jarandilla de la Vera 1:25,000
- IGN 652-IV Campillo de Deleitosa 1:25,000

- IGN 730-III Montánchez
  1:25,000
- IGN 830-111 Hornachos
  1:25,000

A good road map for getting around Extremadura is Extremadura – Castilla-la Mancha – Madrid Michelin Regional Map 576.

HEALTH AND EMERGENCIES

There are no major health risks in Extremadura. There are non-venomous, timid snakes but you are unlikely ever to see one. There are also scorpions: do not move stones or rocks or put your hands in dry stone walls. If stung by a scorpion, do not panic – it is painful but not fatal. Go to a health centre for treatment to avoid infection. Wasp and bee stings are no more dangerous than at home.

None of the walks in this book are perilous, but anyone can have a fall or an accident. In case of emergency, call 112. If you know your GPS location simply give it to the call centre. Rescue from the higher peaks is by helicopter; for non-emergencies walk into a local health centre and you will be seen. Minor problems are treated free of charge at health centres but you should be prepared to show your European Health Insurance Card (EHIC). (British people can apply for an EHIC here: www.gov.uk/european-health-insurance-card; those from other EU countries should consult the relevant government website.) Pharmacies also deal with minor injuries.

Consider taking out general-purpose travel insurance that covers walking activities before you leave home.

DOS AND DON'TS

- Never, ever light a fire in the countryside.

- Take all your rubbish with you (but fruit peels and organic waste are fine to bury).

- If you go through a closed gate, close it behind you. In general, leave gates as they are found.

- If walking through an area grazed by cattle, just walk quietly and calmly. The cows will be used to walkers but may be protective when they have calves. There should be no bulls on any public paths. Do not walk with dogs.

- Do not worry about farmers' dogs. Aggressive dogs will be tethered; the rest will be bored looking after sheep. Never raise a stick to a dog as it will become confused. Just walk on calmly.

USING THIS GUIDE

The 32 walks in this guide are grouped under three headings: the Northern Sierras, the Central Sierras and the Southern Sierras. Within each part the sub-sierras run from west to east. Each walk has its own information box with starting and finishing points, how to access these by car and where to park. (Information about travelling by bus in the region is given in the introduction under 'Getting around'.) The information box also covers the distance of the walk, an estimated walking time, accumulated ascent and descent and a short description of the terrain encountered. The walks vary between 6km and 19km and all but two are circular. A table in Appendix A summarises the walks to help you choose.

Some walks can be linked together to form routes of up to 28km (see Appendix B for a table of linked walks). All involve some ascending and descending but not mountain climbing – they are all definitely walks!

Each walk is described in detail and is accompanied by a map at a scale of 1:50,000, which shows the route and significant landmarks or features. These are shown in **bold** within route descriptions to aid navigation. A few notes on natural and historical information and what to look out for along the way are also included.

The following are definitions of English words and often-used phrases in route descriptions:

- **Lane** – usually in reasonable condition, made either of concrete or compacted stone and earth. Normally near a population centre and is for use by vehicles, horses, bikes and people.
- **Track** – made of almost anything and encountered mainly in the countryside. Wide enough for transport suitable for the terrain, plus horses, bikes and people.
- **Path** – anything from granite-paved or very rocky to grassy or earth. Much narrower than either a lane or track and is for horses, donkeys and people.
- **Stream bed** – dry or wet, depending on rainfall during the previous winter.
- **Wall** – dry stone unless otherwise stated.

A word about names

Wherever possible, names for sierras, rivers and roads are the ones that appear on the most up-to-date maps. However, some names have been chosen to reflect common usage and do not appear on maps other than in this book.

THE NORTHERN SIERRAS: THE SISTEMA CENTRAL

Returning to Gata with the Torre de Almenara in the distance (Walk 3)

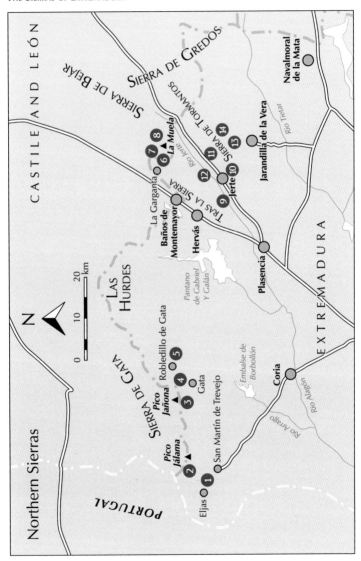

SIERRA DE GATA

WALK 1
San Martín de Trevejo and the Sierra de Eljas

Start/Finish	San Martín de Trevejo
Distance	19km
Ascent/Descent	710m
Time	6hrs
Terrain	Village streets, rural lanes, earth tracks over moorland, footpaths occasionally paved with granite, cobbled woodland track
Max altitude	1058m
Map	IGN 573-111 Eljas 1:25,000
Refreshments	At San Martín de Trevejo and Eljas around the squares
Access	By car: reach San Martín de Trevejo via Plasencia to Coria on the EX-108, or the adjacent motorway. Then take the EX-109 to Moraleja, the CC-3.1 to Cilleros and the CC-3.2 to a junction on the EX-205. Turn left and San Martín de Trevejo is signposted on the right.
Parking	On the CC-1.1 in a parking area on the right opposite the café/bar 'Enigma' and before the entrance to San Martín de Trevejo.
Waymarks	White and yellow flashes
Spring water	One spring just before San Martín de Trevejo
Note	The footpath is vague in places; a compass may be useful. Do not walk in times of poor visibility.

A classic sierra walk. It follows an ancient communication path, the Camino de Navasfrías, over the Sierra de Gata to the Puerto de San Martín, which links Extremadura with Castile and León. The start is on a series of small lanes and a minor road. Once Eljas has been reached, the walk passes through an extensive Pyrenean oak wood followed by a long gentle ascent through wild boulder-strewn moorland to the Puerto de San Martín. Then it

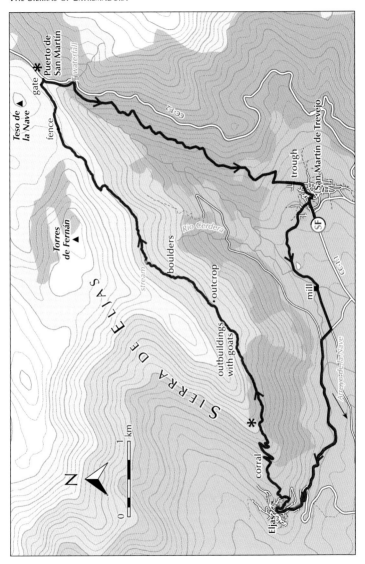

is downhill all the way to San Martín de Trevejo through woods of Spanish chestnut and Pyrenean oaks.

There are many opportunities for spotting flowers and birds, especially near the many small waterfalls and water channels on the high sierra. In autumn the colours in the two woods are glorious.

There is no shade on the exposed sierra between two distinct woods, and the Calzado Romano is uneven in places and can be slippery when wet.

Face the 'Enigma' café/bar and turn right to walk towards San Martín de Trevejo. At the Y-junction the main road bends to the right; do not go that way, but walk straight on down Calle Entrada al Fuente.

Take the second left turning at a small square. This is Camino del Convento. Cross over a crossroads and walk all the way down. The lane bends right past an outbuilding with a waymark, on the right. Just after a utility post with a waymark on the left is a junction before the Convent of San Miguel, now a hospedería. At this junction, turn left.

Walk on this wide concrete lane with generous verges dotted with trees. ▶ After 1km, turn right at a junction to cross a stream by a concrete bridge with crenellated sides and wooden railings. (Over the bridge, on the right, is a **mill** restored as a modern dwelling.) Continue for another 600m to make another right turn at a crossroads with agricultural buildings to the left. Within 200m of this there is a T-junction.

Turn left onto the Carretera de Eljas de San Martín de Trevejo, CCV-61: a quiet back road that does take occasional local traffic. It winds steadily up to Eljas but is shaded by trees, with views to the left becoming extensive as the lane ascends. Come to a Y-junction on the edge of the village of **Eljas**; turn right and follow the main road as it hairpins up to the Plaza de la Constitución. ▶

From the square, with the town hall on your right and the church on your left, walk ahead. At the T-junction, turn left up the ramp, then immediately right up Calle

The Sierra de Eljas is on the right, and to the left are meadow views across a wide shallow valley to the Sierra de Cachaza beyond.

Take on more water from one of the bars, if needed.

de Emigrante. At the T-junction with Calle Folnu turn left, then right. Look ahead for a sign saying 'Calle Cantonis'. Go straight up this tiny road to the right of the sign and turn first right into Calle Orienti – another tiny road but with picturesque, ancient houses. Go straight up this road, ignoring all junctions.

At the end of the road is a T-junction with Calle Forca; turn left onto a wider road. Walk ahead to reach the top of village, still with houses on the left. Reach a Y-junction, to the right of which is a map of walking routes in the area.

On the left are views of the valley and Valverde del Fresno. The sierra lies ahead.

Turn right onto a concrete track as it goes up and bends left. ◄ The track becomes rougher but continues to ascend. Pass a white and yellow waymark on a rock to the right. At a small open space, ignore the gate on the right. Turn left to a gate with a notice in Spanish: '*cierre gracias*' (shut thanks). A waymark on the right pillar by the gate reinforces your direction.

Beyond the gate is a granite-paved path going straight ahead. This continues, with long grassy and earth breaks, all the way to the Puerto de San Martín. This path is the ancient Camino de Navasfrías; it is a wild, uncultivated

On the Camino de Navasfrías

part of the sierra but it is not barren. Walk straight ahead on the paved path and pass a small stone-built **corral** on the right. At a large boulder there is a definite bend, right, to start the zig-zags upwards, steadily but not steeply, with views over the valley on the right becoming more extensive. ▸ As the path reaches a summit, take one last look behind at the **view** of Eljas and Valverde.

The path goes over the top to the other side of the sierra and enters a wooded area. Pass granite boulders, reassuring waymarks and glimpses of the Sierra de Cachaza through the trees on the right. As the path narrows and becomes a bit rough, come to and go through a gate.

The walk enters the thickest part of the wood with trees on both sides of the path. Pass a gate on the left but do not go through it. Ahead, on a big boulder on the left, is a waymark. Pass another gate tucked in on the left but don't go through it. Continue on the path to come to yet another gate, which opens on the right side. Go through this one.

Reach a Y-junction but ignore the tiny path, right, that plunges into the wood. The trees start to thin; reach a gate

Granite boulders with Pico Jálama behind

Already there are birds and hawks to be spotted – depending on the time of day.

with a waymark on its right gatepost and go through it. The trees end on the left and the view is of granite boulders and low-growing shrubs. Trees continue on the right and the path is now rough and boulder-strewn.

Come to an old gatepost with no gate, followed by a gate made of bedsprings, usually open. Go through these. There are two little gates, right, and some small outbuildings. Usually there are **goats** here, and occasionally the goatherd.

Ignoring the two gates, emerge at an open meadow. The path is clearly defined by granite paving, and ahead is the summit of Pico Jálama (Walk 2). Occasionally the path becomes compacted earth but it is clear as no grass grows on it. Keep Pico Jálama as a vague point of orientation – it should be ahead and sometimes a bit right. Ahead and slightly to the left are jagged outcrops called the Torres de Fermán Centeno.

> Many legends surround **Fermán Centeno**, who was a knight from Cuidad Rodrigo to the north of the Sierra de Eljas. He was involved in local power struggles between various factions and seized the defensive castles of Eljas and Trevejo in 1474. He then aspired to take over the western part of the region, which was vital to the defence of Spain against the Portuguese. Today he is known as a legendary bandit who terrorised the local people and hid out in these 'towers'.

This part of the sierra has a wild, primitive aura but is pretty in spring with colourful flowering bushes.

Just after a distinctive **outcrop** of granite on the right, cross a water channel, with glimpses of San Martín in the valley below. Come to a strange but distinctive area of giant rounded granite **boulders**, possibly tumbled from the sierra on the left and eroded over centuries. The path bends left to go through the middle of the boulders and then bends left again. ◄

Reach a **stream** with stepping-stones, after which it becomes hard to pick the way and the path disappears. Veer left; the path appears again and climbs towards the jagged outcrops once more. This is an isolated and

solitary place although cattle may be chewing content-
edly on the higher slopes.

The path, now very rocky, crosses more water channels. (If walking after a lot of rain, it may be boggy in
places.) The ground becomes grassier with boulders
strewn around randomly. The path becomes a tiny dirt
line with a few granite slabs; it comes and goes but keep
Pico Jálama slightly to your right to be sure of staying in
the correct direction.

Over to the right the minor road, CC-193/CCV-12,
comes into view. The Puerto de San Martín is not far
away. The path comes to an inverted Y-junction where it
is joined by a path from the left. Continue right on the
joined path, which now makes a track.

Walk through a very open area with rounded rocks,
pasture, ferns and flowering bushes. Reach a **fence**, turn
right and follow the track, with the fence on the left. The
fence goes off to the left as the track bends right and goes
towards the tree-covered hillside ahead. It narrows and
becomes granite-paved and winds its way down between
the flowered, but rocky, side of the sierra, left.

*On the Calzado
Romano*

Come to the head of the valley with impressive **views** down. Reach a **gate** and go through it: this is the area of the **Puerto de San Martín** and there are information boards and signposts. ◄ Facing the main road, turn right to find the track to San Martín, which for the next 4km runs through beautiful Spanish chestnut and Pyrenean oak wood.

The next part of the walk is waymarked with white and yellow.

The granite-paved track is ancient and had the name **Calzado Romano**, literally meaning 'Roman Shoes'. It is a communication route that links San Martín de Trevejo with towns and villages in Castile and León. Considering its age, it is remarkably well preserved with thousands of original granite paving stones. However, it is thought that it is unlikely to have been laid during Roman times but is more a medieval construction.

Ten minutes into the wood there is a cascading **waterfall** on the left. The path becomes a bridge here as the water flows under the track down to the right and the valley below. Further on, occasional water channels cross the track but these are easily negotiated.

As the track descends, the woods thin and you come to an open rural landscape with San Martín visible below and right. At a T-junction turn right, then turn left to drop down into the outskirts of the village. Pass a **water trough** on the left with clear running water; a good place to 'wash up' before seeking refreshments in San Martín.

To get to the Plaza Mayor, walk ahead and at a Y-junction turn right. (There is an information board here about the Calzada Romano.) Follow this street, Calle del Puerto, as it becomes Calle de la Iglesia and reaches the main square of **San Martín de Trevejo**.

To get back to the start point, walk down Calle el Concejo, turn right down Calle Cordero and turn left into Calle del Fuente, which becomes Calle Entrada al Fuente and goes straight back to the car parking area.

WALK 2
Pico Jálama

Start/Finish	Picnic area on the CV-193 between San Martín de Trevejo and El Payo
Distance	9km
Ascent/Descent	540m
Time	3hrs
Terrain	Woodland tracks, rough tracks, rough footpaths, soft earth footpaths
Max altitude	1487m
Map	IGN 573 Gata 1:50,000 (only partly helpful)
Refreshments	In nearby San Martín de Trevejo
Access	From San Martín de Trevejo on the CV-193. The start is on the left of the road approximately 5km from the village.
Parking	At the start
Waymarks	Signposts, cairns, granite markers
Spring water	One marked spring on the descent
Note	There may be cows grazing but they are used to walkers. Do not walk with dogs.

This walk is rewarded with amazing views in all directions from the summit. The first part of the ascent is through mature pine woods on an easy track; the next part is on a small footpath through low-growing flowering bushes and past rocky outcrops, the way marked with numerous cairns. A well for storing snow and ice is impressive but faintly derelict.

The summit is a place to enjoy with a picnic and binoculars. There are birds of prey, huge eroded granite boulders, flowering bushes and butterflies. Afterwards, the descent is on a footpath marked by cairns and then a wide track. The views on the descent are extensive.

The majority of this walk is not in Extremadura but in Castile and León. The summit, Pico Jálama, is in Extremadura and is the highest peak in the Sierra de Gata at 1487m.

From the picnic area, walk 200m on the road, back in the direction of San Martín until just before the signpost

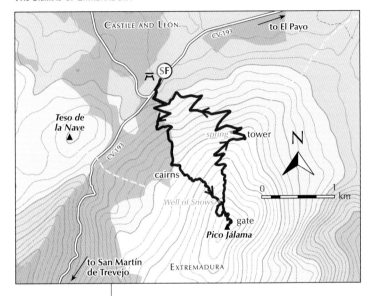

on the right indicating Navafrías and Portugal. Cross the road. On the right, in the bushes and fallen in recent times, is a signpost for Pozo de las Nieves (Well of Snows) 2.8km.

Go through an entrance indicated by two impressive gateposts and cross a cattle grid. Enter the pine wood, turn right and follow the rough, wide track going slightly uphill. The track makes the first of several zig-zags by bending sharply left. After a few meters go through a low swing barrier which normally stands open.

Reach a T-junction and follow the main track as it goes around to the right. (To the left is where the return rejoins the track.) The track zig-zags, becomes rougher and narrower and ascends. The zig-zags stop as the track goes straight ahead and gets much steeper. Continue to ascend as the track becomes narrower and enters a deeper part of the woods. Go straight over a small round clearing and ascend a hillock. The path then makes a decisive bend to the left. ◄

Ahead is a view of the sierra slope covered in bushes with granite outcrops. Behind are views of Salamanca province.

Ignore a wide junction on the left and follow the track as it bears right. On the horizon up ahead and to the left is a line of high rocky outcrops, and to the left of these are tall pine trees that end abruptly: this is the site of the Well of Snows. The track continues to ascend and becomes very rocky, and you come to a lone pine tree on the left. Just after this are groups of **cairns**; this is where the walk leaves the track. ▶

At least eight cairns are visible from the track.

Turn to face the cairns. Continue the walk by going from cairn to cairn: from each one you should be able to see the next, and mostly the next two. Keep as much as possible to the old granite-paved footpath that is visible between the flowering bushes. The going is up and the cairns are very regularly spaced, mainly balanced on large granite boulders so they are visible above the bushes. Keep going up, following both path and cairns.

Come out at a more open area and the cairns are ahead and left. The path goes between tall pine trees. Looking left, you can see both the path and the cairns. It's quite steep now with large boulders to negotiate. Tall pines grow in clumps of twos and threes but the little path continues.

Follow path and cairns to the left and below a rocky outcrop and trees. Walk up to the trees; the wooden fence around the **Well of Snows**, nestling in the trees, is already visible. The path arrives at the back of the well, through a gap in a low wall with cairns on either side. Turn left to reach the information board (Spanish only).

THE WELL OF SNOWS

Before the invention of the refrigerator, the collection, storage and sale of snow was an important source of revenue. In winter, local people would climb the mountain ranges and roll the snow into balls of ice; they would put an oak branch through the ball, allow it to freeze overnight and then carry the ball over their shoulders down the mountains to a specially built '**well of snows**' (*pozo de las nieves*). The balls were stored in the well, tamped down into disc shapes and every few metres were covered with straw. In the summer months the ice was cut, wrapped and transported all over the region for the preservation of food and the chilling of drinks.

The views looking south are of Hoyos, and to the left can be seen Pico Jañona (Walk 3) and the Torre de Almenara (Walk 4).

From the well, continue all the way around to the right and look ahead on a small footpath. There is a metal gate in a fence; go through and follow the small granite markers to the left – not the right – to climb towards the summit. (At one point there is a junction on the left but this is where the return from the summit rejoins the path.) Ascend in zig-zags on the footpath guided by the markers. Near the top, go through a second metal **gate**, turn right and explore the **summit** area where there is a geodesic marker. ◄

Retrace your steps through the **gate** to reach the junction. Turn right and follow the footpath as it descends in a fairly straight direction. Pass through a fence where it is tied up to allow access (this is marked by a cairn). The path goes through a narrow gully with bushes and large rocks on either side, occasionally nearing a fence over on the right. Continue downwards past boulders with cairns on them – although the path is easily defined.

Pause to admire the view to the south of Pico Jálama summit

Reach a fire-watch **tower** on the right. The footpath ends and a series of zig-zags on a well-made wide track

begins. At the end of the first descent, just before the track zigs to the right, there is a **spring** on the left. Ahead is a fine view of the Sierra de Eljas.

On the descent path with the Sierra de Eljas beyond

Continue the descent, ignoring any junctions. Enter the pine wood once more, passing a fire break on the left and an open area on the right. The track bears left and reaches a Y-junction; go right and down. Pass back through the low metal barrier to reach the cattle grid and gateposts. Cross over, turn right to cross the road and arrive back at the **picnic area**.

WALK 3
Puerto de Castilla and Pico Jañona

Start/Finish	Plaza de la Constitución, Gata
Distance	16km
Ascent/Descent	800m
Time	6hrs
Terrain	Village streets, granite cobbled tracks, dirt tracks, rough footpaths
Max altitude	1353m
Map	IGN 573 Gata 1:50,000
Refreshments	Good range of restaurants and cafés in Gata
Access	From Hoyos or Villasbuenas de Gata on the EX-205, turn at the junction for Ciudad Rodrigo. After a few metres turn right at the sign for Gata on the CC-6.1.
Parking	On the side of the CC-6.1 near the Ermita del Humilladero
Waymarks	Signposts, white and yellow flashes, cairns, low granite markers
Spring water	Numerous
Note	There is little shade on the tracks; very hot days should be avoided. There may be cows grazing near the water pool below Pico Jañona but they are used to people. Do not walk with dogs.

A glorious ramble over a pretty part of the Sierra de Gata. The walk goes relentlessly upwards for the first 6km but the ancient granite cobbled track passes many points of interest. There are granite crosses, springs of water, the ruins of a hydroelectric system, the Hermitage of San Blas and unfolding views.

The easy walk on the dirt track from the Puerto de Castilla to Pico Jañona passes through open areas swept with thousands of flowering bushes and views every step of the way. There is a site of archaeological interest, granite outcrops, birds of prey overhead and the view from Pico Jañona to come. Once the track rounds the head of the valley there are views towards the hermitage and down to the valley.

The final part of the walk is a delightful zig-zag path, guided by cairns, down the wild sierra side through flowering bushes, copses of trees and granite outcrops. Altogether a stunning experience.

Walk back to the Ermita del Humilladero on the left and take the street opposite, Calle del Humilladero. Keep on that street to reach the side of the church. Turn right at the sign for the square and then turn left to walk into the square.

Face the town hall in the Plaza de la Constitución. Walk around the town hall, keeping it on the left. Turn

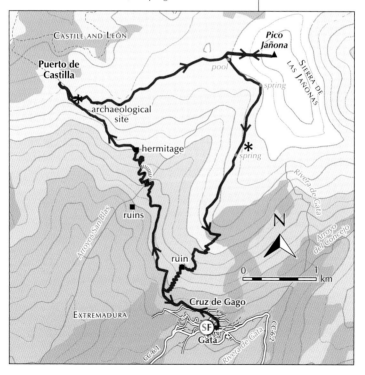

left into Calle Negrón past a drinking water fountain on the left, and reach a crossroads. Go straight on into Calle Virgin del Puerto and follow this small street as it bends to the left and ascends sharply to leave the village where the street ends and a granite cobbled track begins.

Come to a few small stone-built buildings on the right, and just after these reach a Y-junction. Keep on the track as it continues to the right, passing the granite **Cruz de Gago** on the right. ◀ Come to a crossroads and go straight on. Pass signposts for Ermita de San Blas and Puerto de Castilla; white and yellow waymarks start at this point, and views of Pico Jálama (Walk 2) are dominant on the left.

Pass a turning on the right with a huge cairn on its left. (This is where the return route rejoins this track.) As the track winds up, on the horizon ahead and left can be seen the path up to the Puerto de Castilla, while a distinctive copse of pines is ahead and on the right, indicating the site of a hermitage.

> In the deep valley on the left are some ruins. These were buildings of a **hydroelectric station** that generated power for the village. Higher up, to the right of the track, was a round water catchment area. A pipe took the water from this area on a series of pillars, built in descending height to create the fall necessary to generate power. The track passes between two of the pillars.

Pass a small open-sided shelter on the right. The track bears left over the **Arroyos San Blas** by way of a stone bridge. From there the track zig-zags towards a **mirador** with a board explaining what can be seen from that point. Continue up and reach the **hermitage**. ◀

Having visited the hermitage, turn right from the gate and continue all the way up to a crossroads with a well-made dirt track. Puerto de Castilla is signposted, 50m ahead. Reach a Y-junction and follow the path to the left (there is a waymark). Reach a wide, open area with a sign, '**Puerto de Castilla** 1150m'. ◀

Look back for views of the village, while on the left the Torre de Almenara (Walk 4) can be seen.

The gates to the pretty hermitage, gardens, fountains and house are not locked; it is a good place to stop for a while and contemplate the silence.

The border with Salamanca province and Castile and León is just here.

Retrace your steps to the crossroads. Admire the extensive **views** and then turn left on the well-made track. The area is covered in flowering bushes, and the height of the track – plus the open expanse – gives tremendous views on the right as the track continues.

The Mirador and the view to the south

Reach a viewing area on the right; opposite is a granite cross, the Cruz de Manuel. Continue to arrive at an information board (Spanish only) on the right explaining an **archaeological site**.

> From this vantage point at 1150m the **site** dominates much of the western Sierra de Gata. Many blocks of fine granite have been discovered hewn from the area and shaped for construction purposes. Numerous walls have been excavated, and eight circular structures of uncertain purpose have also been found. Ceramics and other artefacts have been discovered but none of them date further back than medieval times.

Ignore the turning on the left and keep to the track as Pico Jañona looms ahead. Come to an open area, on

Drinking water is from the spout inside the small stone construction – not from any other spout. It's cool and delicious.

the left of which are several metal gates. Further left is a metal gate slightly apart from the others; go through this gate. Turn right onto a track that goes straight up and reaches the top of Pico Jañona.

The climb is only 600m but is very steep and without shade. The views, however, are rewarding. There is a fence at the top but it is not necessary to go over to gain the **summit**. Afterwards, retrace your steps to come back through the gate at the bottom of the climb, and walk ahead to reach a **pool** of water for animals. ◀

The track bears around the head of the valley and is visible ahead in the distance. As it descends it becomes rougher. Pass a **spring** on the left, then Las Dehesillas **spring** also on the left; both are drinking water. Across the valley there is a view of the hermitage within its pine trees.

The track bends left and reaches two cairns on the right with a gap between them and a soft earth footpath leading away. Take this turning and follow the path and the cairns. The path is occasionally paved with granite and is clear but the cairns are a guide. (Do not be tempted to leave the path and reach the next cairn by going to it diagonally. As zig-zags occur the next cairn

The pool below Pico Jañona

may be to the right or left rather than ahead; just look carefully and follow path and cairn.) It's a fabulous part of the walk.

Reach a stone building, now a **ruin**, on the left as the path bears right, and arrive at a T-junction. Take the right option. (The left goes to a finca gate.) The path now becomes a rough track that once took vehicles up to the finca. Zig-zag down to join the granite cobbled track by a huge cairn on the right. Turn left and retrace your steps to the square and well-deserved refreshments in **Gata**.

The drinking water fountain at the bottom of Calle Negrón

WALK 4

Castillo de Almenara and the Sierra de las Jañonas

Start/Finish	Plaza de la Constitución, Gata
Distance	10km
Ascent/Descent	450m
Time	3hrs
Terrain	Village streets, granite cobbled tracks, earth tracks, rough footpaths
Max altitude	997m
Map	IGN 573 Gata 1:50,000
Refreshments	Good range of restaurants and cafés in Gata
Access	From Hoyos or Villasbuenas de Gata on the EX-205, turn at the junction for Ciudad Rodrigo. After a few metres turn right at the sign for Gata on the CC-6.1.
Parking	On the side of the CC-6.1 near the Ermita del Humilladero
Waymarks	Signposts, white and yellow flashes, cairns, low granite posts
Spring water	Numerous spouts and wells of water, which the town hall has deemed drinkable
Note	There are stretches of the walk with little shade. Avoid hot days.

The walk leaves the village of Gata on a narrow granite footpath, the Camino la Manforta, and climbs through deep, deciduous woods with the valley of the Rivera de Gata on the right. There are numerous small streams within the woods and these run year-round. The climb out from the woods and towards the castle ruins continues over open areas covered in low-growing bushes – especially broom and retema. The views from the castle are 360° and show a whole sweep of the Sierra de Gredos to the east. The return is on a dirt track which passes through pine woods interspaced with granite outcrops.

Walk back to the Ermita del Humilladero on the left and take the street opposite, Calle del Humilladero. Keep on that street to reach the side of the church. Turn right at the sign for the square and then turn left to walk into the square.

Face the town hall in the Plaza de la Constitución. Walk around the town hall, keeping it on the left. Turn left into Calle Negrón past a drinking water fountain on the left, and reach a crossroads. Turn right into the continuation of Calle Negrón, and come to a junction on the left with signposts and an information board in Spanish and English. Turn left here to follow the Camino de Manforta, a granite cobbled track, as it ascends past agricultural fincas. ▶

There is a view of the castle ahead.

The woods along the Camino la Manforta

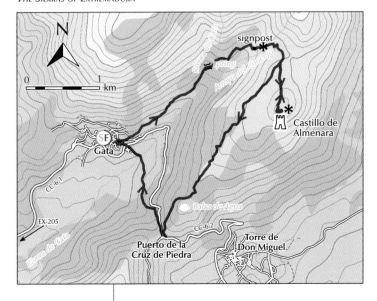

Once past the last of the fincas the track narrows and enters woods of deciduous oak, chestnut and pine. Falls of water cross (or go under) the path to run into the **Rivera de Gata** in the valley on the right.

Reach a Y-junction, go right as indicated by a signpost and continue through the very pretty wooded valley. Reach a wooden **bridge** on the right, cross over it and follow the signposts left. After 20m is a good **spring** of drinking water.

The path continues but is rougher and narrower and winds away from the river. Reach a stream that flows in a channel on the path, but there is enough room to walk on one side (in season). Come to a makeshift wooden gate and slide through it. ◄

On the right is a view of the castle.

Come to a small Y-junction just after the gate: take the right option and continue on the path. Reach a metal gate on the right; the path goes to the left of the gate. Continue, still in the woods, to cross a small bridge. Just after this, the path makes a 90° turn to the right over a stream and then goes straight up, zig-zagging through low flowering bushes to ascend and reach a lone **signpost**, indicating right. ▶

The path, clear and stony, goes through head-height bushes and past copses of trees. As it turns right the castle can be seen once more and the views are 360°. There are cairns, but these are unnecessary as the path continues in the direction of the castle.

Reach a T-junction with signposts on a well-made dirt track and turn right onto the track. Within a few metres, reach a junction on the left with a signpost, '800m to the castle'. Follow the dirt path, passing a signpost on the left for a fountain at 120m.

The dirt path becomes a constructed granite path with small steps. Beware: these are trip-traps on the way up and down. Near the top of the climb the path zig-zags to reach the **castle**, which is really just a ruined pentagonal tower.

This defensive **castle** was constructed by the Moors and its name, Almenara, mean 'fortress' in Arabic. It is made of stone and lime, with ashlars in its five

The views from here are superb, with the whole sweep of the Sierra de Jañonas stretching from left to right behind the signpost.

The Castillo de Almenara sits at the highest point of the walk and gives 360° views

corners. The only remaining architectural feature is a window on the south side. Remains of the round bulwark can be seen in front of the door, from where the tower was accessed by a ladder, as a form of drawbridge; this made attacks difficult and added a defensive element to the tower.

It is possible to walk all around the tower. There are information boards and tremendous 360° views.

In autumn the bracken and ferns turn deep orange to show off against the dark green of the pines. ◄

Retrace your steps to the wide dirt track and the signposts, and turn left. Reach a cattle grid and cross over it. The track initially has no shade but soon enters into a pine wood dotted with giant granite boulders and rocky outcrops. Views of the sierra can be glimpsed on the right through the trees, and the village of Gata is below and right. The descent through the woods is gentle and quite lovely. ◄

Ignore a track on the left and reach a T-junction, where you turn right onto a small lane that is part concrete, part dirt. Pass the **Balsa de Agua**, which provides drinking water for Gata, sat in the high grassy banks on the left. Continue the descent to reach an information board on walks in the Puerto de Perlas area and a Y-junction. Make a U-turn to the right and continue to descend.

Reach a tarmac road, the CC-6.2. Cross over into a wide space and a Y-junction. (This area is the **Puerto de la Cruz de Piedra**.) Ignore the wide track on the left and take the right track downwards. (There is a waymark.) Follow the track down to cross a bridge over the Rivera de Gata once more. There are information boards about the GR10-E7 long-distance walk.

Ascend into the village via the street on the left, which crosses a second bridge. Walk all the way up the street to reach the Ermita del Humilladero on the left. Retrace your steps to the square in **Gata** for refreshments or turn right to return to the car.

WALK 5

Robledillo de Gata and Ovejuela

Start/Finish	Car park just outside Robledillo village on the CC-7.2
Distance	16km
Ascent/Descent	960m
Time	6hrs
Terrain	Village roads, dirt tracks, earth footpaths – some occasionally paved with slate
Max altitude	1008m
Maps	IGN 574 Casar de Palomero 1:50,000 and 551 Martiago 1:50,000
Refreshments	Robledillo has good cafés; Ovejuela has a few bars
Access	By car: make for Coria, then Moraleja and the EX-109 towards Hoyos. At the Hoyos T-junction turn right and reach Robledillo de Gata on the CC-6 and CC-7.
Parking	In a car park at the T-junction off the CC-7 before entering the village
Waymarks	White and red flashes (part of the GR10-E7), white and yellow flashes
Spring water	None en route
Note	Do not walk if the weather is poor or at times of high water.

This ancient and remote place with unspoiled mountainsides covered in mixed evergreen and deciduous trees is wonderful for walking. The low-growing bushes flower profusely in spring. High waterfalls cascade down deep valleys feeding narrow, fast-flowing rivers strewn with boulders. Extremadura's highest waterfall, Chorrituelo de Ovejuela, is a memorable sight. The scattered villages have houses that are stone-built and crammed higgledy-piggledy down steep valley slopes. Many of them are of historic interest and importance. Both Ovejuela and Robledillo de Gata are worth exploring – the latter village is classed as one of the most beautiful in Spain.

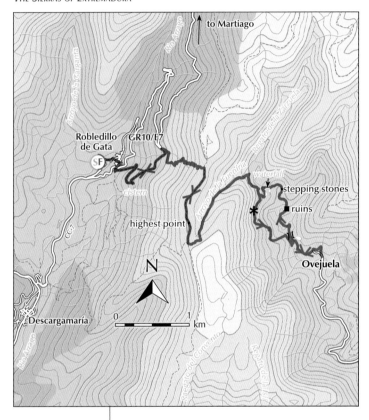

Walk into Robledillo de Gata along the street named Puente and turn right into Calle Congosto. Then turn right into Calle Barrero. At the end of the village come to a crossroads and go straight over. Turn first left into a wide lane – the CCV-7 – which ascends steadily with views of the village, left and below. It hairpins right then left, passes an open **cistern** of clear water on the left and continues upward.

The lane bends left and left again. At a green sign for the **GR10-E7**, turn sharp right onto a rough track.

The GR10 is a **long-distance route** in the Iberian Peninsula that connects Valencia on the Mediterranean Sea with Lisbon on the Atlantic Coast. It is 1600km in length. The E7 is a long-distance route that travels through Hungary, Slovenia, Italy, France, Andorra and Spain. An extension through Portugal is at the planning stage; it will then connect the Black Sea to the Atlantic Ocean. Currently the distance is measured at 4330km.

Cross a small stream on stepping-stones and start to go up in wide zig-zags. Reach a second green signpost for the GR10-E7, on the right. The track, more rutted now, continues up in tighter zig-zags. Come to a bare, rutted slope and pass a small black sign for 'Robledillo de Gata' on the left before arriving at a T-junction with a wide, well-made lane. Turn right.

Follow the wide lane with views of villages in the eastern Sierra de Gata and woods of deciduous oaks, holm oaks, pine and Spanish chestnut trees on the way to the **highest point** of the walk. Just over 1km later, pass

Houses in Robledillo de Gata

59

a lane on the right. Just opposite, left, is a track entering the woods. Take this track. (As an extra guide, look for a marker stone with a white and red waymark that is in the middle of the track just before the entrance to the wood.)

The descent winds gently through hundreds of flowering bushes – stunning in spring but also beautiful in autumn. Reach a stone on the right with a waymark and go right. (Do not go left as it descends the valley too early.) The path ahead meanders and hairpins and continues downwards gently. Keep going – this part is nearly 2km long. ◄

There are stunning views left and ahead.

Eventually reach a junction with a path going left, which is where the return route rejoins this path. Go right to follow the slate-lined path that comes out from the trees; it is wide and well-made and descends along the side of the valley with extensive **views** to the left. (The village is visible, left and ahead, and mountains stretch in the distance.) Follow the path until it bears very sharp left to zig-zag downwards to a **bridge** and a natural **pool**.

To explore Ovejuela, turn right and pass the pool, keeping it on your right. Ascending into the village past olive groves, come to a sanctuary and pass it on the left. Walk ahead on a tiny street between two stone buildings to reach an open area; explore **Ovejuela** then return to this point and retrace your steps back to the natural pool and the bridge.

Once back over the bridge there are arrows both left and right. Turn right to ascend a small footpath with the river on your right. Go straight at the top of the first climb and descend slightly; the footpath bends left and goes down to reach the river. Cross using the stepping-stones and then turn right. Follow the waymark on the left to turn left up quite a well-made path, and ascend. Follow the path past **ruins** of a stone building on the left – the path is littered with stone and slate – and at the top of the climb turn left, following a sign for 'Veleha Chorrituelo,' the waterfall.

Follow the path, visible in the distance, with the river below and left (note the small picturesque falls). The valley walls become steeper and higher, and there are likely

The highest waterfall in Extremadura, the Chorrituelo de Ovejuela

to be birds of prey high up the valley sides. Drop down to the river and cross it using the **stepping-stones**. Turn right and continue on the earth footpath, following the waymarks and passing a tricky stretch of up-ended slate boulders.

Cross the river on stepping-stones once more and follow the path sharply up to the left. Climb up to view the spectacular **waterfall**, the Chorrituelo de Ovejuela, and its natural pool. ▶ Afterwards, descend sharply to cross the river again, this time on rocks, stopping for a better view of the waterfall.

With your back to the waterfall and the river on the left, retrace your steps slightly to pick up a small footpath that ascends the side of the valley. Follow the waymarks and enjoy views of the waterfall, behind and right, as the climb goes up. It's very, very steep in places, but not long.

The path goes through a deep pine forest with many flowering bushes. At the top of the climb, come to a T-junction with arrows and instructions: right goes to Robledillo de Gata, even though it says 'Prohibido' (pro-hibited). Turn right and retrace your steps all the way back to **Robledillo de Gata**.

The crystal-clear water falls from a height of 50m down an almost vertical slate valley wall. It never runs completely dry.

SIERRA DE BÉJAR

WALK 6
La Garganta and El Nevero

Start/Finish	Opposite the town hall, La Garganta
Distance	7km
Ascent/Descent	220m
Time	2hrs
Terrain	Village roads, single lane road, dirt tracks, open meadow, earth footpaths – a few paved with granite
Max altitude	1268m
Map	IGN 576 Cabezuela del Valle 1:50,000
Refreshments	In the pleasant La Garganta bars that also do tapas
Access	By car: from Baños de Montemayor, follow the sign for La Garganta on the CC-16.1 and wind up the road to the village. One acute hairpin – the others are easy.
Parking	In the small square opposite the town hall
Waymarks	Signposts, white and green flashes
Spring water	Two fountains at the parking area near the start
Linking routes	Walks 7 and 8

A short but pretty walk with great mountain views. The walk goes through woods of pine and deciduous trees including oak and chestnut. In spring there are flowering bushes with broom still yellow into June. Wildflowers are everywhere, especially in the meadows. Songbirds abound but raptors circle overhead. There are mountain views of the Cordillera del Molinillo y del Hornillo and Sierra de Béjar, forested hillsides, deep valleys, views of distant villages and lakes, a wolf trap and, very often, grazing animals.

Walk up the only main road, Calle San Juan. Just after the road bends to the right and leaves the village there is a junction on the left and a signpost indicating the start of the Valle del Ambroz walk to Hervás, PR CC-37. Take this

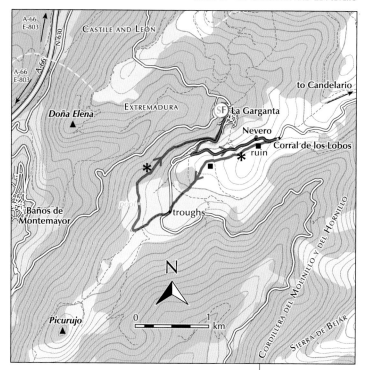

turning left and ascend the narrow footpath occasionally paved with granite.

Come out on the La Garganta–Candelario single lane road, turn left and walk in the wide verge of this road to reach a pine wood, passing a signpost and information board on the left. Down in the pine wood, on the left, is **El Nevero**, a 'well of snows'. (For information about the function of a well of snows, see Walk 2.)

Continue along the road, coming out from the pines. On the left is an open space with a stone-built seating area, some information boards and a wooden-fenced wolf trap, the **Corral de los Lobos**, disused for many years (see Walk 7 for details). ▶

From this point the view of the mountains of the Sierra de Béjar, snow-topped for much of the year, is spectacular.

Link to Walks 7 and 8

The Corral de los Lobos is the pivotal point at which Walk 7 and/or Walk 8 can be added to this route. From here, pick up the directions for either of those walks, follow them to arrive back at the Corral de los Lobos, then continue on this walk by following the directions below.

Turn right on the single lane road to retrace a few steps. Cross the road, turn left and then immediately right/ahead on a wide earth track going towards a ruin on the horizon. (There is a signpost 'Sendero Local El Nevero SL-CC-97 Cordel Berrocal Picquojol'.) Ignore the small track that goes down and left.

Ascend, looking back for views, to reach the **ruin** where there is a waymark on the wall. There are new views ahead as the summit is reached, with the Gabriel y Galán reservoir in the distance. The track descends; ignore the left turn that goes to a finca, and reach a crossroads with a weekend house on the left. Go straight ahead and come to a makeshift gate.

Go through the gate (closing it behind you: it keeps animals in and not people out) and continue through an open meadow. Reach a crossroads with a signpost for Hervás going left and the sign for 'El Nevero' going across the open space. Follow the track ahead, visible as it crosses the meadow. Go straight over a dirt track that crosses the main track and reach a gateway with a lane beyond. Go through the gate and turn left; there is a waymark on the left post and on the lane. On the right, pass consecutive granite water **troughs**.

Just after the troughs, take a small rough track going right and down. Come to a Y-junction and keep right, then reach a second Y-junction and keep right again. A signpost is visible ahead. At the signpost there is also a white and green post; turn sharp right here and hug the wall on the right. Pass over rough ground with large flat boulders and flowering shrubs to find a narrow earth footpath with the wall still on the right.

The path may be boggy (there are stepping-stones) and there may be other boggy bits for the next 100m.

This path reaches a ruined house on the right with a **pool** edged with granite on the left. ◄ Pass through

deciduous copses and areas of flowering bushes with splendid **views** on the left. La Garganta comes into view, ahead and left. The path reaches a concrete and compacted earth track as it enters the village, and then reaches a road. Turn left and follow the road down to the square and the car in **La Garganta**.

Meadow with flowers in late May, with the snow-capped Sierra de Béjar beyond

WALK 7
La Muela and the forest track

Start/Finish	Opposite the town hall, La Garganta
Distance	14.5km
Ascent/Descent	640m
Time	5hrs
Terrain	Village roads, single lane road, dirt tracks, woodland tracks, rough granite paths, earth footpaths – some occasionally paved with granite
Max altitude	1605m
Map	IGN 576 Cabezuela del Valle 1:50,000
Refreshments	In the pleasant La Garganta bars that also do tapas
Access	By car: from Baños de Montemayor, follow the sign for La Garganta on the CC-16.1 and wind up the road to the village. One acute hairpin – the others are easy.
Parking	In the small square opposite the town hall
Waymarks	Signposts, cairns
Spring water	Two fountains at the parking area near the start, and Fuente Piluca on the climb to La Muela
Linking routes	Walks 6 and 8
Note	Do not undertake this walk in poor visibility.

La Muela, a huge granite outcrop in the Cordillera del Molinillo y del Hornillo, is the focus for this diverse walk, which crosses into Salamanca province and the Autonomous Region of Castile and León. En route, the usual flowering bushes feature strongly in season – especially yellow broom and pink Spanish heath. The views from the high point of the walk, facing north-west, are spectacular, as is the view in the other direction to the Sierra de Béjar. Vultures circle the skies, especially during the lambing season.

Much of the return walk goes through pine woods with giant granite boulders strewn between the trees. Watch out for red foxes in the woods.

Walk up the parking space, passing two fountains with drinking water. Near the top, reach a multi-junction, look

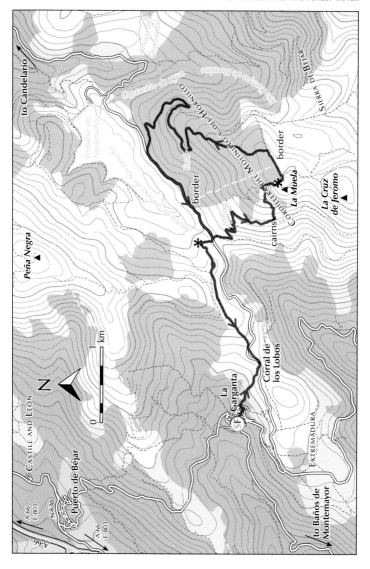

Above La Garganta

ahead to see the sign for Calle Venero and bear right. Continue to a concreted track, go straight over and follow the rough track, keeping in the middle, to reach the **Corral de los Lobos**, a wolf trap, with low stone walls.

Sheep have always been important in Extremadura, and La Garganta is on the Cordel del Berrocal, one of the *trashumancia* routes (on which sheep were moved between winter and summer pasture) through the Sierra de Gredos. This **wolf trap** is a reconstruction of one that existed here for centuries; the walls are low and the interior floor level considerably lower than the surroundings. The trap was baited, and once the wolves jumped in to reach the bait they could not get out and were dealt with in the usual manner.

Ahead and slightly left is La Muela with the Sierra de Béjar behind. Impressive!

Also here is a single lane road which links La Garganta to Candelario in Salamanca province. ◀ Cross the road to turn left and walk on the soft, wide verges. Follow the path across open ground to come to the road once more; cross over and ascend the rough track ahead.

Ignore the small path that joins the track from the right, and pass two pine copses on the right. Come to a track crossing and turn right, then within a few paces come to a T-junction where you turn right again. At the next Y-junction choose either path as they meet again within metres. Note the superb outcrop of granite rocks high on the left, while ahead is a **view** of the Navamuño reservoir.

Reach a T-junction and turn right; the track drops to the road ahead, but just before meeting the road take a small path left, cross the road and ascend the track on the other side.

Come to a Y-junction and take the rougher track on the left, ascending. The track becomes wider and less rough as it ascends and zig-zags through a deep pine forest where there are huge granite boulders scattered among the trees.

Pass Fuente Piluca, a **spring** with drinking water, and reach a T-junction where you keep right to stay on the track. Approximately 700m after the junction, the top of La Muela appears on the left. Just as it appears there are **cairns** on the left indicating where to leave the track and ascend through rough ground with low bushes.

The small path is clear but the cairns are essential. ▶ Near the top, do not be distracted by cairns going to the left – they are for another walk. The 'correct' cairns bear right and lead the path around La Muela, with a pine forest coming into view on the right. (On the left are another group of giant rounded boulders.) Keep the pine forest on your right and follow the path ahead.

Reach a track at a T-junction – a continuation of the left track not taken at the T-junction earlier – and turn right towards La Muela. The track is rough and ascends around **La Muela** with stunning **views** into the valley. Keeping La Muela on your right, reach a wide opening in a fence and go through it. ▶

With a pine forest on the left, continue on the track, which bends to the left. Within 150m of the fence, cross the **border** into Salamanca province and the Autonomous Region of Castile and León. Reach an open meadow with

The next cairn should always be visible.

This is the point at which it is possible to link to Walk 8.

View of the Navamuño reservoir

a fence on the right looking into the valley; beyond (in season) is a view of snow-melt cascading down mountains, creating waterfalls. The roar can be heard across the valley.

Reach a Y-junction, go left and enter a deep, resinous pine forest. Keep to the track, which is well-made but occasionally descends steeply as it winds downwards, ignoring any junctions. As you walk through the forest, views of the mountains appear on the right. Flowering bushes grow where the trees are thinner, and as the track descends views of the Navamuño reservoir appear through the trees.

There are many small falls of water coming from left to right under the road, and the views are all on the right.

After about an hour of walking, reach the La Garganta to Candelario single lane road. The reservoir is across the road; turn left and cross the road to walk on the wide verge closest to the water. ◀

Reach a sign that reads 'Esta en Cáceres Bienvienidos' (You are in Cáceres Welcome) and cross the **border** into Extremadura once more. Pass the La Muela turning to the left and turn right to reach the **Corral de los Lobos**. Retrace your steps to **La Garganta** (or add part of Walk 6 to make a longer adventure).

WALK 8

Valley route to La Muela

Start/Finish	Opposite the town hall, La Garganta
Distance	15.5km
Ascent/Descent	700m
Time	4½hrs
Terrain	Village roads, single track road, dirt tracks, earth footpaths – some occasionally paved with granite, low flat granite boulders
Max altitude	1605m
Map	IGN 576 Cabezuela del Valle 1:50,000
Refreshments	In the pleasant La Garganta bars that also do tapas
Access	By car: from Baños de Montemayor, follow the sign for La Garganta on the CC-16.1 and wind up the road to the village. One acute hairpin – the others are easy.
Parking	In the small square opposite the town hall
Waymarks	Signposts, cairns
Spring water	Two fountains at the parking area near the start, and Fuente Piluca on the descent from La Muela
Linking routes	Walks 6 and 7

The ascent towards the summit of La Muela is along the valley side of the Cordillera del Molinillo y del Hornillo. The views over the Ambroz valley – world-famous for the autumn colours of its deciduous trees – are spectacular. Views of the Sierra de Béjar from the southern part of the walk are also dramatic. The descent is through woods with views to the north-west. Underfoot are the usual flowering bushes; overhead are eagles. It is a phenomenal walk.

Walk up the parking space, passing two fountains with drinking water. Near the top, reach a multi-junction, look ahead to see the sign for Calle Venero and bear right. Go straight on to reach a concreted track; go straight over it and follow the rough track until a vague three options present themselves.

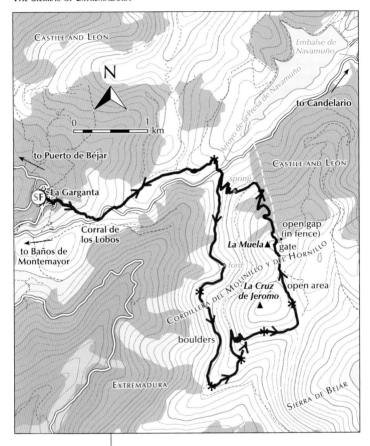

From here, 200m to the right on the road, is the Corral de los Lobos – the link point with Walks 6 and 7.

Choose the rough footpath on the left with a low dry stone wall to its left. The path gently ascends and comes out on the Candalerio to La Garganta single track road with a view of La Muela ahead. ◄ Turn left and walk on the verge of the road for about 25m, then leave the road to turn left onto a rough track going up.

Ignore a small path that joins the track from the right, and pass two pine copses on the right. Come to a track crossing and turn right, and within a few paces reach a T-junction. Turn right again. At the next Y-junction choose either path as they meet again within metres. (Ahead is a **view** of the Navamuño reservoir.)

Reach a T-junction and turn right. The track drops down to the road ahead, but just before meeting the road take the small track left, cross the road and ascend the track on the other side.

Reach a Y-junction and take the option on the right (a well-made dirt track). The views, a constant companion along this part of the walk, are on the right over the Ambroz valley extending down towards Hervás. On the left is the side of the Cordillera del Molinillo y del Hornillo with bushes and pine trees higher up. The track winds up and down and, on the left, opposite a fold in the sierra side on the right, the top of La Muela comes into view.

Water coming from left to right crosses the track at a **ford**. The track starts to climb quite steeply and bends naturally to the left. Arrive at 360° **views** and enjoy one of the best sights in Extremadura, then continue to pass enormous granite **boulders** on the edge of the track on the left.

Reach a Y-junction. Turn left, bear left and then left again, making a loop that ascends all the time. ▶ On the right, down in the valley, is a small farm building with a round stone corral. Reach a Y-junction where the right turning only goes to the entrance to the farm, and keep left. As the loop turns back the way the track came, but higher, the **views** are extensive – almost 360°.

There are stunning views of the array of mountains in the Sierra de Béjar ahead and right.

The **Sierra de Béjar** is considered by some geographers to be the most westerly part of the Sierra de Gredos. Although the sierra lies in Castile and León, its southern edge borders Extremadura. Many walks in the Ambroz valley give extensive views of its peaks.

Just after the junction and view there is a fence on the right that bends right into the side of the sierra. Just

The Sierra de Béjar from La Muela

there is a small path with a cairn to its left; this is a short-cut and goes straight up, rather steeply, in the direction of a pine forest, to meet the longer track within 300m.

If taking the longer track, however, do not turn right on the small path but continue ahead. Come to a T-junction and turn very sharp right to start a series of zig-zags upwards, and meet the short-cut as it comes up on the right, indicated by cairns.

Continue ahead on the track with a pine forest on the left and a deep valley with **views** of mountains beyond on the right. The track gets rougher and goes up at a point where huge rounded granite outcrops can be seen ahead. It makes a right-angle bend to the left, goes up and continues with the forest on the left. ◄ After bending left again, with a view of rocky granite outcrops rather like smashed meringues, the track bends left once more and ascends, now narrower.

The views on the right are of villages in Salamanca province and mountains beyond.

Reach an **open area**. A path, narrow and rough, can be seen ahead going to the left of La Muela (the biggest smashed meringue). There are cairns at its start to the left and right; descend, then ascend this path. The path comes to a more open area where there are huge boulders, narrows again and picks up a fence on the right.

There are more cairns now but they are not needed – the path is clear.

At another open area, the obvious path stops and large flat granite slabs and low boulders take over – take care as these are slippery when wet. Follow the cairns, keeping La Muela on the left. (The route does not go around La Muela but passes to the right of it.) Where the cairns indicate left, do not go left; instead take a well-trodden path going right and pick up new cairns within metres.

Reach a fence on the right, with **La Muela** on your left, and go through a spring-loaded green metal **gate**.

Immediately turn left on the low rock, then continue ahead. Walk straight ahead over the large flat boulder to come out onto a track, where you turn right. Within metres reach a Y-junction; turn left to reach an open gap in the fence and go through it. ▶

At this point it is possible to link to Walk 7.

Continue on the track, which is quite rough and descends very steeply at times. Come to a T-junction, go right and continue downwards to reach Fuente Piluca on the right – a **spring** that is drinking water. Arrive at the La Garganta–Candalerio road, cross over and retrace your steps to **La Garganta**.

Granite rocks just below La Muela

SIERRA DE GREDOS

WALK 9

Cascadas Nogaleas in the Montes de Tras la Sierra

Start/Finish	Puente Viejo, Calle Hernán Cortés, Navaconcejo
Distance	7km
Ascent/Descent	470m
Time	3hrs
Terrain	Concrete lane until the last cherry orchard, earth footpaths, occasional granite steps, occasional exposed tree roots on footpaths
Max altitude	810m
Map	IGN 576 Cabezuela del Valle 1:50,000
Refreshments	Bars, cafés and restaurants in Navaconcejo
Access	By car: reach Navaconcejo on the N-110 signposted from Plasencia. The road goes through Navaconcejo and parking is easy to find.
Parking	Anywhere in Navaconcejo and in the triangle by the start
Waymarks	White and green flashes (SL-CC 33)
Spring water	None en route
Note	The first part of the walk has little shade, so walk early on hot days.

A pretty walk with numerous waterfalls set in a deciduous wood. The initial ascent gives impressive views back to Navaconcejo and the Sierra de Tormantos behind the town. From the walk's high point, the descent meanders on a path alongside the River Nogaleas, which joins the Jerté river in the town. There are many viewpoints to a stunning series of more than a dozen waterfalls and pools, each with their own charm. Within the shady woods are wildflowers and flowering bushes, in season, and much bird activity, especially in spring. However, it is the waterfalls that are the real highlight of this walk. Spectacular after periods of rain.

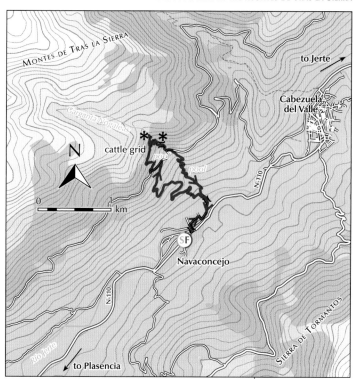

Start by crossing over the Puente Viejo on the N-110 at the eastern end of Navaconcejo. Just over the **bridge** on Calle Puente, come to a junction on the right with a sign for Calle Nogaledas and Ruta de Nogaleas. Go right. At the end of the street is a yellow sign; turn right. Just by Calle Adolfo Suarez on the left, look up to see waterfalls descending from high up the small river valley in the foothills of the Montes de Tras la Sierra.

Pass a play park on the right. The street narrows considerably and becomes rough before reaching a small **bridge** on the right, but do not turn here – this is where the return rejoins the street. Go straight on instead.

White and green
waymarks appear
at intervals.

The concreted lane climbs out from Navaconcejo, giving views of the village and the mountains behind every time it zig-zags up. ◄ As the lane winds steeply up, there are glimpses on the right of waterfalls. Reach a Y-junction and go right, keeping to the narrow concrete track to reach a T-junction with a small tarmac road. Turn left.

Reach a junction with a track going to the right and up; take this track and enter a deciduous oak wood on a track that is now earth. The views are fabulous and the track continues to ascend. Come to a junction with a very small path going off to the right. (There is a small **cattle grid** and two waymarks.) Leave the main track to take the earth footpath, right, and go deeper into the woods.

Reach a Y-junction, down and right, with a wooden fence and signpost. However, first go straight on to reach a **viewpoint** within an area of huge boulders and a waterfall. Afterwards retrace your steps to the junction, now on the left.

The earth footpath descends but there is a rope handrail to help in the steepest places. Reach a T-junction where the left option leads to a **viewpoint**. Go left, then retrace your steps and continue straight on at the junction. Descend steps cut into the granite to pass enormous granite boulders and come out at a metal **bridge** and a big waterfall. Cross the bridge and continue on the path through the woods, using the handrail as appropriate.

Come to another T-junction and this time go right for the viewpoint, then retrace your steps and continue straight ahead to reach another T-junction. Go right for one more viewpoint before the path reaches a T-junction with a tarmac road. Turn right for a few metres to view a natural **pool** and waterfall, then turn left to retrace your steps.

Cross the road and on the right is a small sign and waymark for a footpath that descends into the woods. The path is made of earth, granite slabs, cut steps and occasionally paved with granite; the river, with its waterfalls, is on the right, and there are glimpses of the village ahead and below.

*One of the waterfalls
that feeds a small
pool near the end
of the walk*

Reach a T-junction: to the right is a viewpoint; to the left is the continuation down to the village. At the next T-junction simply go right. After some earth steps edged with wooden logs, reach another T-junction where right is the viewpoint, left is the continuation of the walk. After this there is another T-junction within metres: go right and continue on the path but beware the tree roots.

There are another two viewpoints, right, and the walk continues, left. At the following junction turn right to reach a pool and waterfall. This time the walk continues from the pool and not back at the junction. Turn left

Goats enjoy the lush grass at the edge of the River Jerte in Navaconcejo

from the pool and go up some steep granite steps to turn right at the junction and continue the walk.

Reach a viewpoint on the right and then the final one, also right. Come out from the woods to cover a short stretch on a concrete lane through cherry orchards. Reach a T-junction, turn right and descend past a small shop on the left selling local products.

Come to the **bridge** where the walk originally went straight on. Cross the bridge, turn left and retrace your steps back to cross the Puente Viejo and arrive back at the car parking area in **Navaconcejo**.

WALK 10

Los Pilones and Puente Sacristán

Start/Finish	Puente Largo, Plaza del Molino, Jerte
Distance	12km
Ascent/Descent	500m
Time	4½hrs
Terrain	Concrete tracks, a stretch of old granite paving, dirt tracks, soft earth footpaths with occasional granite slabs, steps, two bridges, water channels, one seasonal ford
Max altitude	832m
Map	IGN 576 Cabezuela del Valle 1:50,000
Refreshments	Bars, cafés and restaurants in Jerte
Access	By car: Jerte lies on the N-110 between Plasencia and Ávila.
Parking	In the wide part of the N-110 as it passes through the village
Waymarks	White and yellow flashes, white and green flashes, fingerposts
Spring water	Fuente Pilones near Los Pilones
Linking route	Walk 11
Note	Do not attempt to cross the Vado Cantares (ford) if the water level is high. The granite boulders are slippery when wet; do not 'chance it' as the water flows strongly here.

This stunning walk in the steep-sided Jerte river valley takes in Los Pilones – naturally occurring granite basins filled with water – as well as seasonal falls of water crossing the path in small channels and long stretches through shady woods. It is best enjoyed after rain when the water is abundant. Conversely, that makes it impossible to cross the *vado* (ford) and link with Walk 11 – an option in drier conditions to make a longer walk.

Start in Plaza del Molino, Jerte, where there are maps and information boards. Cross the bridge, Puente Largo,

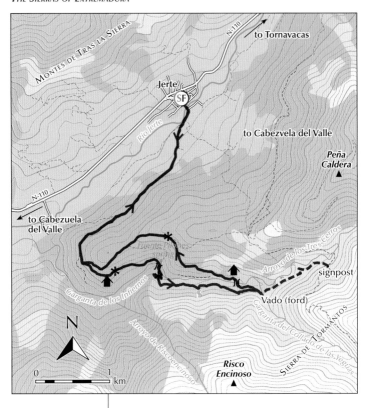

over the river and turn right. At a T-junction keep right to continue on the track, then reach a Y-junction and go left (the right goes to the Interpretation Centre). At a little Y-junction the track bends right; at another Y-junction go left. (There is a signpost 'PR-CC 2 Camino en Flor'.) Come to another Y-junction where the path on the right goes to the Interpretation Centre and Los Pilones is left. Keep left.

Across the valley the Chorrero de la Virgin, a high waterfall, can be seen, in season.

Come to the **Refugio del Escribano** on the left and a picnic and viewing area on the right, where there are more information boards. ◄ Continue on the track to reach a cobbled section and another picnic area on the right, then reach a Y-junction with yet another picnic area on the right, also with information boards, and the Fuente Pilones spring. Go right to descend to the **bridge** over Los Pilones. (There are granite steps and guide rails.)

LOS PILONES

Centuries ago, boulders brought down from the higher mountains in snow-melt became trapped in the narrows. The action of water currents created a circular movement that gradually eroded the soft underlying granite into basin-like shapes that are now small pools. These are Los Pilones – a *pilon* being a basin for a fountain or a drinking trough for cattle.

Once over the river, continue on the granite steps as they ascend, keeping to the right side of the wooden fence. ▶ Come to a fingerpost – 'Puente Nuevo SL-25' – and turn right to walk up the steps. The path makes a sharp bend to the left and the ascent is steep. Then the path bends right to go back in the direction it came from, but higher. Reach an open area with signposts indicating walk options and great views, and turn left onto a well-used earth footpath.

Do not climb the rocks.

The footpath continues with only a few ascents and descents, following the river valley. ▶ Cross the first of many granite channels that allow water to fall from right to left to rush down the valley and join the Jerte. Use stepping-stones as necessary.

The high mountains are all around. On the right the Sierra de Tormantos rises steadily into the distance.

Reach an area where the path has granite steps to aid the ascent. (In season there is a small **waterfall** on the right.) Pass a sign on the right for 'Fuente del Camino' – but there is no indication the water is drinkable. There is a view of cherry orchards on the other side of the valley to the left, and in the valley is a small well-made building – the Refugio de Pescadores – and a bridge, Puente Sacristán, over the river. On your left is a small footpath going down to the bridge, but do not turn left here. The walk continues ahead.

Come to an information board about Vado Cantares, a ford in the river coming down from the right to join

Los Pilones

the Jerte in the valley. Walk on a few metres to reach the vado. There are waymark posts at either side indicating where it should be crossed, but if the water level is high, do not attempt a crossing.

Link to Walk 11
If the vado can be crossed, and if desired, continue on the path to a signpost and Puente Nuevo, from where you can pick up the directions to return to Jerte from Walk 11.

If the vado cannot be crossed, return to the information board and walk down the small track on the right – not the path on the left, which returns to Los Pilones. This small track drops down to the **refugio** and **bridge**, which can be seen ahead. The path near the bottom of the track is a bit meandering but only for a few metres.

Cross the bridge and turn left on a soft earth track. Ascend to reach a staggered junction with two turnings left and one right; keep ahead on the track, ignoring other junctions. The track ascends around the curve of the valley behind the cherry orchards seen from the viewpoint earlier. ◄ Reach the junction with Los Pilones once more and retrace your steps back to **Jerte**.

On the left are stunning views of Los Pilones in the valley.

WALK 11

Jerte to Puente Nuevo in the Sierra de Tormantos

Start/Finish	Puente Largo, Plaza del Molino, Jerte
Distance	16km
Ascent/Descent	570m
Time	5½hrs
Terrain	Initial 1.2km on concrete tracks then dirt tracks, soft earth footpaths with occasional granite slabs, one bridge, one seasonal ford
Max altitude	958m
Map	IGN 576 Cabezuela del Valle 1:50,000
Refreshments	Bars, cafés and restaurants in Jerte
Access	By car: Jerte lies on the N-110 between Plasencia and Ávila
Parking	In the wide part of the N-110 as it passes through the village
Waymarks	White and yellow flashes, blue bands, fingerposts
Spring water	Fuente de los Linares on the Vía Pecuaria
Linking route	Walk 10
Note	Do not attempt to link to Walk 10 by crossing the Vado Cantares (ford) if the water level is high. The granite boulders are slippery when wet; do not 'chance it' as the water flows strongly here.

This spectacular walk in the Jerte river valley climbs sharply out from the village, past cherry orchards to reach a deciduous wood. The track and then earth path continues to ascend through the woods, reaching the highest point of the walk before descending to the Puente Nuevo. The walk is best enjoyed after rain when the water is abundant but, conversely, that makes it impossible to cross the vado and link to Walk 10. The return is through a deep, mainly chestnut wood, and the final part back to Jerte is along an old Vía Pecuaria – a track traditionally used for moving animals. In spring the valley sides are covered in wildflowers and flowering bushes, especially lavender. In autumn the deciduous trees are spectacular colours.

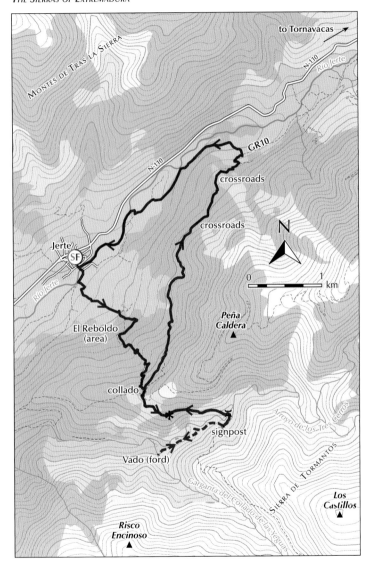

Start in the Plaza del Molino and cross the bridge, Puente Largo, over the Jerte. Turn right and reach a junction on the left, signposted 'Puente Nuevo 4.6km'. Turn left up the concrete track, which ascends sharply, passing fig and cherry orchards. As the track winds upwards, views unfold of Jerte and the mountains behind, the Montes de Tras la Sierra.

Reach a signposted junction and go left. The track levels a little and passes through more cherry orchards before reaching a junction by a small house whose upper storey backs onto the track. Turn right at the waymarks and signposts. The track enters the shade of an oak and chestnut wood; pass a sign on the left for 'La Garganta de los Infiernos Parque Natural'.

> The Jerte river, which never runs dry but is full with snowmelt water in spring, crashes down from the mountains along its narrow valley known as **La Garganta de los Infiernos** – The Narrow Pass of Hell. Ironically, the natural park is a walking paradise.

Come to a junction and turn right at the signpost. The concrete stops just after the junction, becomes compacted earth and continues through the woods. Reach a junction and turn left to pass through an area called **El Reboldo**. The track narrows and becomes rougher but it is very pretty. The going up is relentless and steep but the trees give shade on warm days. A few zig-zags to help with the ascent.

Where the track bends naturally on the left, pass a sign for 'Fuente de Jarandilla' – but although there is water, it is not drinking water. Come to a junction and go right on a much rougher track to reach a Y-junction. The track ahead is overgrown; turn left on a small, signposted footpath that ascends into the woods. The earth footpath with occasional granite rocks winds its way up through the deciduous woods with glimpses of views over the Jerte valley on the left.

The footpath reaches the wider track, 'Ruta Carlos V (PR CC-1)', at a T-junction. Turn right, then left, to ascend

View over the Jerte valley from the path

The 360° views are over the Jerte valley and down to the river. The spectacular Sierra de Tormantos towers above the path and fills the view from left to right. On the other side of the river, on the right, the path taken in Walk 10 is also clearly visible.

the last metres to reach **Collado** de las Losas, the highest point of the walk. Turn right to head for the information boards that are clearly visible, then turn left on the earth path to start the descent to the bridge. ◄

Come to a Y-junction, turn left and enter a deciduous oak wood on a soft earth path that runs fairly flat. Reach a small Y-junction, leave the path and descend right. The path narrows and has long stretches of granite slabs. There is a steep drop on the right down to the Jerte but the path is wide enough to walk easily – but with care. Reach the **bridge**, Puente Nuevo.

Although this bridge is called the **New Bridge** it was built over 460 years ago. When, in 1556, Carlos

V, Holy Roman Emperor, King of Spain and most of the New World, decided to retire because he was wracked with gout and old at 56, he chose Extremadura – sensible man. His ultimate retirement place was Yuste Monastery but he travelled there in stages. From Tornavacas to Jarandilla de la Vera he was carried in a sedan chair by local men who fought for the honour. The bridge was built so that the Jerte river could be crossed at this point. The signposted route is walked by hundreds of people every November; it's 28km long and reaches heights of over 1500m.

Link to Walk 10

At the bridge there is the option to cross over and pick up the small path on the right that ascends on granite steps. Follow the path to reach a **signpost**. Left is up to Jarandilla (18km) and right is the Jerte Interpretation Centre and the SL-25. Follow the path, right, to the **Vado** Cantares. If it is fordable, there is the option do the Los Pilones walk in reverse or drop to Puente Sacristán and return to Jerte that way. See Walk 10.

Puente Nuevo seen from the Vado side

Walking through the chestnut woods outside Jerte

From Puente Nuevo retrace your steps back up to **Collado** de las Losas. Take the junction from the collado back down the Ruta Carlos V – it is signposted. Continue on the waymarked track for the next 4km through deep chestnut and oak woods, watching for exposed tree roots. The descent runs more-or-less straight; ignore all junctions but at a pronounced Y-junction, go left.

Reach two **crossroads** and at both of them go straight on. At a vague T-junction, go left and at the next T-junction, also go left. Reach a Y-junction just after farm buildings and turn left to Jerte at the signposts, including one for the **GR10-E7**.

The track, the Vía Pecuaria, at first a little rough and later a wider dirt lane, goes back to Jerte with just one junction. At the Y-junction, turn right. Walk on a dirt lane through shady woods, passing Fuente de los Linares (drinking water). Reach Puente Viejo, turn right and come to the square in **Jerte** once more.

WALK 12

Puente los Papúos in the Montes de Tras de Sierra

Start/Finish	Puente Largo, Plaza del Molino, Jerte
Distance	6km
Ascent/Descent	270m
Time	1½hrs
Terrain	Concrete tracks until the last cherry orchard, then earth tracks and footpaths
Max altitude	836m
Map	IGN 576 Cabezuela del Valle 1:50,000
Refreshments	Bars, cafés and restaurants in Jerte
Access	Jerte lies on the N-110 between Plasencia and Ávila
Parking	In the wide part of the N-110 as it passes through the village
Waymarks	White and green flashes
Spring water	None en route
Note	If walking in July and August, set out early or late in the day.

This lovely little walk, with its series of waterfalls, is not as spectacular as the Cascadas Nogaleas (Walk 9) but has its own enchantment. For most of the walk the river is visible within the deciduous woods of oak and alder through which it flows. Cherry orchards are planted on either side of the track until these give way to uncultivated land of wildflowers and flowering bushes. In season the waterfalls at the bridge, the Puente los Papúos, are delightful. The view on the ascent is of the Sierra de Béjar and on the return takes in Jerte with the Sierra de Tormantos behind the village. It is most enjoyable after periods of rain when the river water is high.

Start from the bridge, Puente Largo, just off Plaza del Molino. Do not cross the bridge but with it behind you, turn right and walk along Calle del Puente. Pass the hospedería on the right and continue up to the **N-110 road**. Cross the road – the Papúos river is on the right (and goes under the road and past the hospedería to flow into the Jerte river).

Just after crossing the road are two information boards about 'La Garganta de Papúos'. Walk straight ahead on the small concrete road, Calle de la Tahona, past a few village houses. Just after the last house is a white and green waymark indicating a right turn onto a concrete track; take this to reach a **bridge** that crosses the river with a waterfall on the left. Just over the bridge turn left and ascend steeply with the river, shaded by trees, on the left.

Keep on the track – the junctions only go into cherry orchards and fincas. Glimpses of the river and the other side of the valley are on the left, and you pass through enormous boulders on either side of the track to come to

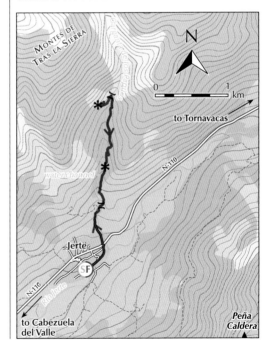

a Y-junction. Left goes a short way to reach an interesting old granite **water channel** and a small waterfall, but the walk continues on the track to the right, which becomes earth with concrete on steeper climbs and zig-zags.

At an inverted Y-junction turn left to come to another Y-junction and turn left again. (There are waymarks.) At a Y-junction with a finca entrance on the right, the track narrows considerably and the soft earth path is shaded by an oak wood. On the opposite side of the valley there are low farm buildings and terraced cherry orchards, while the river can be seen below and the towering mountains ahead. ▸

Reach an open area. Waymarks indicate to go left, and on the left is a tiny path with another waymark. This path heads towards the river and the bridge, which can be seen in the distance. The path winds its narrow way through low bracken and bushes to reach the **Puente los Papúos** where there is an open area and in season there are impressive falls of water. Cross the bridge and take the track to the left for 100m as it bends right, and turn for a **viewpoint** of the bridge and falls.

Retrace your steps back to **Jerte** with spectacular views of the Sierra de Tormantos behind the village on the way down.

Jerte and the Sierra de Tormantos from the cherry orchards

Just a few degrees east of north, 5.75km as the crow flies, is Calvitero – the highest peak in Extremadura at 2400m.

93

WALK 13
The Jaranda valley

Start/Finish	Outside the Parador, Jarandilla de la Vera
Distance	14km
Ascent/Descent	656m
Time	5hrs
Terrain	Tarmac street, concrete road, dirt track, earth footpath, cobbled lane
Max altitude	915m
Map	IGN 599-II Jarandilla de la Vera 1:25,000
Refreshments	Bars, cafés and restaurants in Jarandilla and Guijo de Santa Bárbara
Access	By car: reach Jarandilla de la Vera via the EX-119 from Navalmoral de la Mata or the EX-203 from Plasencia. Follow the signs for the Parador or Centro Urbano.
Parking	Avenida Don Joquain Ruiz or other side streets around the Parador in the centre of Jarandilla de la Vera
Waymarks	White, yellow and green flashes, directional signs, fingerposts, cairns
Spring water	None en route. Bottled water is available to buy in Guijo de Santa Bárbara.
Linking route	Walk 14

The walk runs alongside the picturesque Jaranda river through woods and rough open ground. A short stretch along made roads passes a wooded mountainside to reach the village of Guijo de Santa Bárbara. There are three bridges to cross and one to visit. Ascents and descents give views of the river below, the mountains above and of both villages. The return follows the old Camino de Santo Nuncio to reach the highest point of the walk, after which the descent is through open meadows and rough ground covered with flowering bushes. There is a deep, deciduous oak forest with a lavender-covered floor and a compacted earth track going back to the river. The final ascent to Jarandilla de la Vera is on a cobbled track.

This is best walked in the spring when the flowers are out and the river is swollen with snowmelt from the mountains.

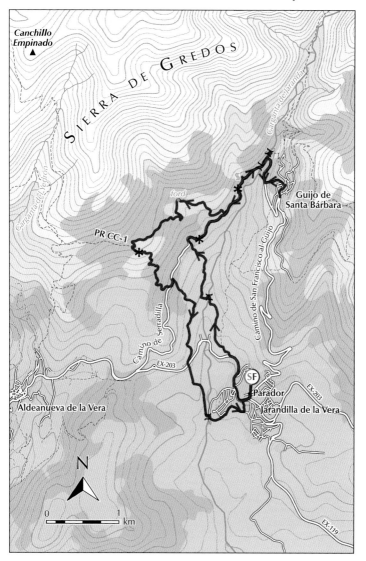

Walk towards the roundabout and the Parador, then walk round the **Parador** with it on the right to pass the tourist office. The street becomes the EX-203 road. Continue around the Parador, passing the park and a garage, and just after the Hotel Rural Robles come to a lamppost on the right with white, yellow and green waymarks and indications to go right on a track. (There are also waymarks for the PR CC-1.) Leave the EX-203 and go right here.

Reach a Y-junction in the centre of which are signs for Guijo de Santa Bárbara, GR 111 white and red waymarks and a post with white, yellow and green waymarks. Turn right up the concrete lane and come to a house on the right. (The concrete lane continues right; it is the Camino de San Francisco al Guijo but it is concrete all the way.) Take the earth track to the left with white, yellow and green waymarks and PR CC-1 signs.

Within metres the track becomes a soft earth footpath. At a Y-junction keep right, and at a second Y-junction stay on the footpath. At a third Y-junction, at an open area with granite boulders and flowering bushes, keep left and follow the waymarks.

There is the first view of Guijo de Santa Bárbara ahead and right.

Reach the Puente de Palos and cross the **bridge**. Once over the bridge, keep straight ahead to come to a T-junction and turn right. ◄ Pass a few rural houses as the track ascends; at a Y-junction ignore the right track and keep left to continue the ascent on a concrete track. By a modern house on the right, meet a tarmac road, the Ctra. de Guijo de Santa Bárbara. Turn right and follow the road, ignoring turnings on both sides.

Down on the right, near the river and a bridge, is a collection of traditional round houses, part of a tourist area served by two gates on the right.

At a pronounced bend in the road there is a fine **view** of Jarandilla and Guijo. The road becomes a bridge over a small stream with a pool at the side and you pass a track on the left with a signpost, 'Camino Santo Nuncio', which is where the return will branch off. For now, pass a 'welcome' sign to the village as the road descends and gives fine **views** of the mountains above. ◄

Come to a lay-by on the left. At the back is a short, narrow footpath that leads to a viewpoint for a towering **waterfall**, which flows under the road to join the Jaranda.

Cross the road where it becomes, in effect, a bridge over the waterfall. As the road continues the river can be seen on the right, while on the left is a tall hillside covered in trees and flowering bushes.

The old bridge and the natural pool near Guijo

Reach a big **bridge** over the river. As the road bends to the right, on the left there is a picnic area with a café – open during holidays – a footpath to a natural pool and a small, picturesque **bridge**. There are also many other footpaths to explore. The road itself continues to Guijo with a sharp right turn, ascending steeply. Take the first lane on the left, about halfway up the ascent, to reach the village.

GUIJO DE SANTA BÁRBARA

Guijo de Santa Bárbara is one of the locations that lays claim to being the birthplace of Viriato, the famous Celtiberian leader who led the Roman army a dance between 147BC and 139BC. There is a statue of him in the village. However, Guijo itself was not founded until 1400, long after the Christian Reconquest in Extremadura.

The Sistema Central mountains protect the village and its 420 inhabitants from freezing winds in the winter and gives the area a milder climate. Guijo is justly famous for its jams – especially raspberry.

Link to Walk 14

On reaching the first of the village houses, take the third turning on the right into Calle Ctra. Nueva. Walk ahead to come to an open area with Plaza Corredores lower down on the right and a car parking area just ahead and right. Straight ahead are two small roads, both going to Jarandilla de la Vera. Left and higher up is a sharp turning going back towards the village; this sharp left turning is the start of Walk 14.

After exploring the village, return to the bridge and walk back up the road to the track, now on the right, to the Camino Santo Nuncio. Turn right onto the camino and stay on the rough concrete track as it winds upwards, ignoring all junctions. There are a few scattered houses and farms and the view on the right is of a wooded hill.

Cross a **ford** and reach a T-junction; go left and take in views of Guijo and Jarandilla. Ignore the two turnings on the left as the road continues to wind round and ascend. Pass between two small houses and ahead and to the right is a farm. Ignore the small track left, and just as the road bends right to reach the farm there is a big, old tree and a track on the left. Take this track and within a few metres reach a T-junction. Go right and within a few more metres come to a track going down and left. (There are signs, white and yellow, '**PR CC-1**, Ruta de Carlos V Fuente de los Pilones'.) Take this track.

Follow the waymarks and occasional cairns all the way down the broad track, which becomes a winding footpath occasionally paved with granite. There are good **views** of both Guijo and Jarandilla, plus other villages in La Vera: Aldeanueva, Cuacos and Jaraiz. The path bends left at a low dry stone wall with a deciduous oak wood on its other side. Stay on the path, keeping the wall on the right and enter the wood, following the waymarks.

At a T-junction with a wide woodland track, turn right. As the track bends left, go ahead on a tiny footpath. Come to another T-junction with another wide track and go right. Reach an open glade; a waymark indicates left but go second left on the wide track. Come out from the

woods on a tarmac lane, where waymarks indicate left. Look for the next waymark on the road and turn right down a rough track.

One of the towers of the Parador

The track meets a dirt road at an angled T-junction. There are signs to turn left (to Puente de Palos), but turn right instead. Follow the dirt road through the woods to meet the **EX-203**. Cross the road straight over and turn left to descend to the Jaranda river. Cross the **bridge**, Puente Parill, and turn right. Within metres turn left up a cobbled track and follow this up past a modern housing estate on the left. At a Y-junction turn right, then first left into Cuesta de los Carros. The **Parador** is across the road at the top of this street.

WALK 14
Guijo de Santa Bárbara and El Trabuquete

Start/Finish	Car park at the entrance to Guijo de Santa Bárbara
Distance	11.5km
Ascent/Descent	840m
Time	6hrs
Terrain	Village streets, dirt tracks, earth footpaths occasionally paved with granite, open meadow with rough pasture, woodland tracks
Max altitude	1475m
Maps	IGN 599 Jaraíz de la Vera 1:50,000 and IGN 576 Cabezuela del Valle 1:50,000
Refreshments	Guijo de Santa Bárbara has bars, cafés and restaurants
Access	By car: from Jarandilla de la Vera follow the signs for Guijo de Santa Bárbara. The two-way road ascends in hairpins but is not difficult.
Parking	On the left at the entrance to the village. Do not drive into Guijo.
Waymarks	Signposts, white and yellow flashes, red arrows, cairns
Spring water	At the hermitage
Linking route	Walk 13
Note	Although the walk is not particularly long, it is tough. Do not attempt to walk beyond the hermitage if the weather is poor, misty, wet or likely to snow.

A varied, challenging and stunning walk. The route ascends relentlessly to the hermitage but the footpaths are winding and easy to follow. In spring the lavender and broom are profuse. From the highest point it is often possible to see birds of prey flying below in the valley – a change from looking up at them. The descent is very steep until the first bridge is reached, then the path is single-file along the sierra ridge with a chance to spot mountain goats hiding in the dramatic rocky valley. The return is alongside the Jaranda river and spectacular all year but especially when the river is high. In addition to the hermitage, there are two *chozos* (traditional shepherd huts) to explore and seven bridges to cross. Take binoculars for the views, birds and mountain goats.

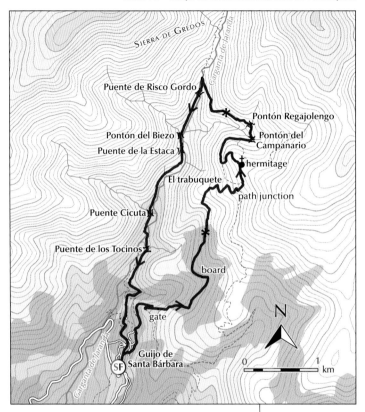

Start in Guijo de Santa Bárbara from the car park. Do not walk ahead to Plaza Corredores, but facing the square, take the street on the far right opposite the car parking area. ▶ Follow the white and yellow waymarks to turn right up Travesia Monje, then first right into Camino del Curato. Then turn left and follow this street away from the village, passing several information boards and a granite water trough on the right. The street becomes a narrower concrete track and the glorious mountain views start from here.

This is where Walk 13 joins this route.

Follow the track around to the right to begin climbing more steeply around sharp hairpin bends. The village quickly recedes and the track comes to a **gate**. Pass through this, turn left and wind up with views of the high mountains on the left. Enter an area of deciduous oak trees.

The still-concrete track rises gently through the trees until it becomes a rough, dirt-and rock-strewn path at a small stream and a sharp left bend. At a junction on the right are waymarks (both white and yellow and red arrows on posts). Go right and come to a wildlife information **board** on the left. At a Y-junction, pick up a path on the right that passes reassuring white arrows painted on rocks.

Continue on the path – you can't go wrong as it's very definite – as it gently rises all the time. Eventually it emerges from the woods to give extensive **views** on the left of the village below and the other towns of La Vera in the distance.

The terrain changes as the trees are left behind. The path is a little rockier and much steeper. The views are more open and the mountains dominate the left side. Keep to the path as it passes through a wide open meadow; there are path options here, but take the more gentle approach and follow the waymark posts and cairns. Ahead, the hermitage and refugio can be seen as a point of reference. Follow the path to the right where there is a red arrow waymark.

Keep going quite steeply upwards with the hermitage in view on the left now. The path joins another one coming from the right at a **path junction** – an alternative path from the village. Bear left towards the **hermitage** and with a final effort reach it and the highest point of the walk.

Every year on 5 August the village celebrates the **Romaria** in honour of Our Lady of the Snows. The villagers walk up to the hermitage and celebrate the day by eating, drinking, playing games and taking part in activities in the area around the hermitage and refugio.

Towards the hermitage

Having refreshed your drinking bottles at the fountain, with the hermitage behind and the view out over the valley in front, turn right and walk down the slope to a red arrow waymark. Turn left and follow the path as it initially loops away from the hermitage and then drops down to the right in a loop. The descent is steep but the views of mountains all around are wonderful.

Pass very high granite formations on the right and continue dropping down the side of the valley. The small river valley of La Garganta del Campanario is on the left, and a bridge is clearly visible.

Reach the **bridge**, the Pontón del Campanario, cross over and bear left. Now comes the most spectacular part of the walk. The path follows, very clearly, the side of La Garganta del Campanario but gains in height gradually. Reach a second bridge, Ponton del Regajolengo, slightly to the right, exploring the traditional chozo (El Campanario) on the left before crossing. Cross the bridge and continue on the path.

It's a small path with a profound 100m drop to the right at times, and bushes to the left that can encroach. Pay

Looking back up the valley from near the last bridge, Puente de los Tocinos

There are birds of prey and wild mountain goats, and the deep valley has many high, imposing rock formations known as Las Costillas (The Ribs).

attention but stop to enjoy the view – often. ◄ Continue on the path carefully as it goes around in a long U-bend, descending all the time. Be careful of the loose rocks and encroaching bushes.

Finally drop down to the River Jaranda and the El Trabuquete part of the walk. Turn left to walk with the river on your right until a **bridge**, Puente Risco Gordo, is reached. Cross the bridge and keep close to the river to continue on the path as it negotiates boulders and a few rough areas. Tucked in on the left, pass the second chozo of the walk. Within 100m the path becomes much clearer and from here it is well-defined all the way down the valley with the water on the left.

Pass Pontón del Biezo and Puente de la Estaca. Reach the El Trabuquete area (signposted) – a favourite spot with locals in the summer. Stay on the path to pass over Puente Cicuta and then reach the **bridge**, Puente de los Tocinos. Cross over and leave the river.

Look back for the last views of the mountains in all their beauty.

Continue gently up a wide track towards the village. The river valley is now on the right and below. ◄ The track bends left and comes to a small copse; turn first right onto a small earth path, which leads all the way back to the **Guijo** via the Camino de la Sierra, Calle la Mata and Calle Ctra. Nueva.

THE CENTRAL SIERRAS: MONTES DE TOLEDO

The Sierra de Montánchez from the Sierra de Santa Cruz (Walk 21)

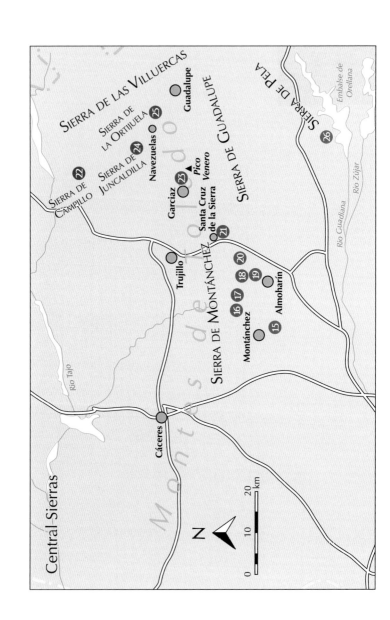

Central-Sierras

Sierra de las Villuercas

Sierra de la Ortijuela

Sierra de Juncaldilla

Sierra de Campillo

Guadalupe

Navezuelas ⑤

㉒

㉔

Garciaz

Pico Venero

㉓

Santa Cruz de la Sierra

Sierra de Guadalupe

Sierra de Pela

Embalse de Orellana

㉖

Río Zújar

Río Guadiana

㉑

Trujillo

Sierra de Montánchez

⑳

⑱ ⑲

⑯ ⑰

Almoharín

Montánchez

⑮

Río Tajo

Montes de Toledo

Cáceres

N

0   10   20
km

SIERRA DE MONTÁNCHEZ

WALK 15
Arroyomolinos

Start/Finish	Arroyomolinos
Distance	13km
Ascent/Descent	570m
Time	5hrs
Terrain	Village lanes, dirt tracks, earth footpaths occasionally paved with granite, riverbeds, streams, low fords
Max altitude	870m
Map	IGN 730-III Montánchez 1:25,000
Refreshments	Bars and cafés in Arroyomolinos
Access	By car: enter the village from the CC-60/CC-117 from the Alcuéscar–Montánchez road. Take the first entrance coming from Alcuéscar/Montánchez or the last entrance coming from Almoharín at the small mill building. Keep left until an open area is reached by two tall communication antennae.
Parking	In the wide open area at the top of Calle Altozano
Waymarks	None
Spring water	One spring three-quarters of the way around
Note	The second climb is particularly steep. Take care when exploring the mill races.

This lovely, but tough, walk has distinctive parts. The first is along a fairly flat lane passing through agricultural landscapes with the Sierra de Montánchez as a backdrop. The next part follows a narrow footpath that climbs through low-growing vegetation and scattered trees. There is a very brief flat track before a steep, rough footpath climbs through deciduous oaks with extensive views towards the east. Next is a short descent to a gentler path, which curves around the sierra before entering into a small chestnut wood. The final part of the walk is a descent in the valley to Arroyomolinos. There are ruined mills and aqueducts to explore, and the chance to see profuse wildflowers in spring and griffon vultures, hawks and kites all year round. The views are many and spectacular. Take binoculars.

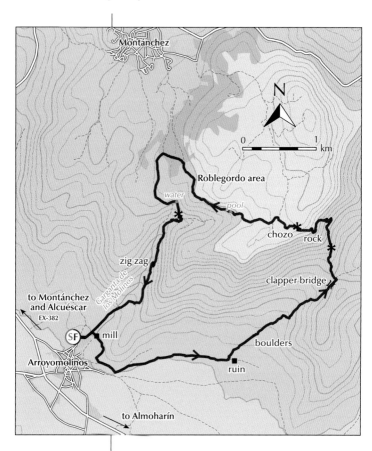

Walk straight towards the two antenna ahead on the concrete road to reach a Y-junction, and go left. Pass a turning on the left and take the one to the right a few paces further on. Walk on the rough track and follow it to pass the ruin of a **mill** on the left.

Cross a small ford, the first of many, and continue as the track winds and narrows. ▸ At a wide space with multiple gateways, the track bends left; come to a T-junction and take the left track away from the village. Walk until a long, grey outbuilding is reached on the right and a red one is straight ahead. There is a junction: turn left onto a wide track to put the red outbuilding on your right.

On the right are views of the villages of Arroyomolinos and Alcuéscar behind.

Follow this wide track with a view of the sierra on the left, crossing occasional low fords and ignoring all junctions. At a substantial Y-junction keep right, and at the next large junction also keep right. Pass a distinctive little house in a finca on the left – it has an arched door and window. Immediately after this finca is a footpath and then another finca, which also has a small building but is currently a ruin. Take the footpath between these two fincas.

The footpath, occasionally paved with granite, is narrow but clear. It winds its way, gradually ascending, parallel to the Sierra de Montánchez on the left. Pass an area

The Sierra de Montánchez

of low granite **boulders** and reach an open area: here the path bends to the right, picks up a dry stone wall on the right and continues ahead. The path meanders but keep looking for the granite slabs.

Come to a wide, clear area with what looks like a riverbed on the right by a dry stone wall. Go diagonally right towards the wall, and just before reaching it pick up the path and follow it ahead through head-high bushes on either side.

In the two fincas on the left are abandoned farmhouses.

The path ascends very steeply, makes a sharp bend to the right and continues relentlessly up. Come to a small, low **clapper bridge** that crosses over the path to allow a water channel to flow under it. ◄ The path continues upwards to reach its summit in a wide area with a T-junction; go left on a level earth track where there is a magnificent **view** down to Arroyomolinos.

On the left are the Montes de Toledo; Cancho Blanco and Cerro San Cristobal (Walk 19) are ahead; a spur of the Sierra de Montánchez is just below and part of Arroyomolinos to the right.

Within 100m come to a decisive bend to the left. On the right are small metal gates: go through these. The footpath ahead climbs the southern side of the Sierra de Montánchez; it is steep, rough and dotted with deciduous oak trees. There are no junctions at all. Start climbing, and at the top of the first climb enjoy the view. ◄

Continuing, the footpath enters an oak wood. Reach an area with planted orange trees and terraces – under the wall of the path is a granite water trough with drinking water but it's not really accessible. Start the first of many zig-zags up, noting on the left a horse-shaped **rock** evocative of the ancient animal sculptures found all over Extremadura.

> The **Vettones**, a distinct Celtiberian tribe, had migrated to the area from northern parts of Europe during the fourth to third centuries BC. They were horse and cattle herders and seasonal trashumante practitioners. They carved enormous animal sculptures – mainly pigs – in granite. These are known as *verracos*, which is Spanish for boar. Many of the megalithic sculptures remain dotted around the countryside but are also to be seen in Cáceres Museum.

Mill race above Arroyomolinos

At the top of all the zig-zags the path becomes level, with walls left and right as well as oak trees. Follow the path but look back for a final **view** before crossing the top of the sierra to gain the view on the other side. ▶

On the right, in a finca, is a chozo – a typical shepherd's hut.

Come to a T-junction and take the track to the left. Ignore another junction left and continue ahead to pass, on the right, a small house. There is a water channel on the right and the track narrows to descend through an area of trees, bracken and undergrowth. (Depending on the weather there may be a low ford to cross.) Chestnut trees start and the village ahead in the distance is Alcuéscar.

As the path comes out from the trees it bends right; walk ahead on the ancient footpath and come to a waterfall and natural **pool**, in season. ▶ The path winds along the side of the sierra through an area known as **Roblegordo**. Ignore junctions on the left, and come to the start of a deep chestnut wood on the left. There is a metal gate alongside with a small path that enters the wood: take this path and follow it through the woods.

On the left is a view of the first of the mill races which are a feature of this valley.

Once out of the woods, come to a T-junction and turn left onto a well-made track. Keep to this track as it winds downwards, ignoring any junctions. Reach a source of

Seasonal waterfall and natural pool

drinking **water** on the left and continue to a Y-junction where a small metal gate sits between the tracks. The left turning (earth) goes up; the right (concrete) goes down and makes a U-turn right. Go right and follow the track as it descends quite steeply in places. There are views ahead of mills and mill races.

Pass a renovated mill which is now a weekend house. Make a small detour ahead to see the mill pond, which has been over-prettified. Continue on the concrete track as it zig-zags to descend more steeply and cross over the stream that feeds the mill pond. Once over the stream, an earth footpath starts.

Follow the path all the way down the valley full of mills and mill races to **zig-zag** at one renovated mill and continue on downwards. As the path descends the valley sides become towering: watch for birds of prey overhead. At the end of the path come out onto a concrete lane and turn right. Cross over a low ford and pass a final mill ruin on the right. Continue down the lane to arrive back at **Arroyomolinos**.

WALK 16
Torre de Santa María to Montánchez

Start/Finish	Main square, Torre de Santa María
Distance	13km
Ascent/Descent	400m
Time	4hrs
Terrain	Village streets, lanes, rough tracks, earth footpaths occasionally paved with granite
Max altitude	740m
Map	IGN 730 Montánchez 1:50,000
Refreshments	Bars and cafés in Torre de Santa María and Montánchez
Access	By car: turn into Torre de Santa María at the sign on the EX-206 Cáceres–Miajadas road
Parking	On the outskirts of Torre de Santa María
Waymarks	None
Spring water	One spring near the top of the climb by the granite troughs

White broom bushes are a feature of this walk in spring. Ancient granite footpaths climb steadily out from Torre de Santa María, and as the path ascends the views become extensive to the east towards the Sierra de Guadalupe. The top of the climb offers an opportunity to walk into Montánchez, explore the historic castle and sample some *jamón* (ham) in the Plaza de España. The return is by footpaths through shady woods with stunning views to the west. The path follows the line of the sierra before descending into cork oak woods and returning to Torre de Santa María.

From the main square in Torre de Santa María, facing the church, look right to see a sign for the Casa de Cultura. Walk down that street, named Calle del Campo. Come to a small open area with two concrete utility poles just ahead and a choice of four junctions: take the first turning on the left.

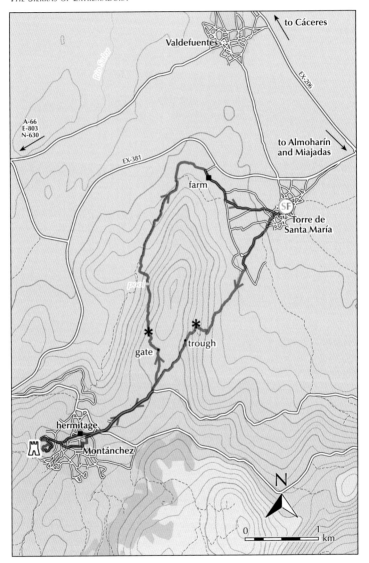

Reach a T-junction and turn right. Within a few paces come to another junction with four options and take the second on the right. Walk ahead, ignoring small junctions left and right, to reach the village outskirts. Just past a row of old houses on the right, reach a Y-junction: turn right up a rough track and continue. Pass a modern low red-roofed house on a finca to the right and come to a Y-junction. Go right, and come to a junction where a fresh water pumping station can be seen on the left of the right turn. Do not go right but continue straight ahead.

At a small clearing go straight ahead on a narrower footpath, which ascends steeply. ▶ The dirt path is not more than 2km long but it does wind very steeply up over areas of large granite boulders and paving slabs. Just before the top of the climb is a granite water **trough** on the right; the water from the pipe is drinkable. On the left of the path is a typical shepherd's hut – a chozo – and views across the valley.

On the left are views to the distant Sierra de Guadalupe.

Come to an open area with a double metal gate on the left – but the path turns sharply right, then bends left and ascends. On the right, pass a modern house, then a copse of oaks and views of Montánchez Castle. Ignore

Vineyards in autumn with Montánchez Castle in the distance

two junctions on the right and keep ahead. Pass a jamón factory on the left, and at the Y-junction go right onto a tarmac lane. Follow the lane until it reaches the outskirts of **Montánchez** and a roundabout. ◀

The detour from Walk 17 joins here.

Cross the roundabout and continue straight ahead. Just before the Guardia Civil building on the left, turn left, then right, then left again into a car parking area. Take the street on the right to walk all the way down to a small square with a fountain. Turn right to walk into the Plaza de España, where you can enjoy a delicious (and expensive) plate of jamón. Afterwards, leave the square diagonally opposite the entrance and follow signs for 'Castillo' up a steep hill. At the top turn left, then left again to reach the **castle**.

> **Montánchez Castle** dates from the times of the Moors who wrested the town from the Visigoths in 713. Alfonso IX reconquered Montánchez in 1230 and strengthened the building to keep it defensive in those turbulent times. It fell into disrepair over the centuries but has recently been undergoing restoration. There are fabulous views from the castle walls.

On the way back down from the castle, walk ahead into the small park just before the right turn down the hill. ◀ Retrace your steps down the hill but do not turn right into the square again; instead keep left, walk under a small arch and turn left down Calle Lectoral Lozano. Pass a small **hermitage** on the left and continue into Calle Gereral Mola. Reach the roundabout, cross over and retrace your steps.

The views from the park are endless.

Just after the jamón factory there is a Y-junction: take the left track and come to a wide open area with three options. Keep ahead to pick up the walk in the pretty lane with vineyards on the left.

Reach a metal **gate** where the track splits in two – one going to the right of the gate and the other to the left. Take the small path to the left and follow it as it goes up slightly and twists through low-growing deciduous oaks.

Reach a granite-strewn ridge and a **view** of Montánchez Castle on the left and behind. At a vague junction by a dry stone wall on the left, veer away from the wall slightly. Keep right to stay on the path, which picks up a wall on the right. The path may be encroached by low bushes but it is well-defined between the vegetation. Pass a metal gate on the left with good views out towards the north, and follow the path as it enters the edge of a deciduous oak wood.

Reach a Y-junction and go left down steep boulders to continue on the path between dry stone walls. ▶ The path descends gently but is steeper at intervals; junctions at this point are often only alternative paths to negotiate tricky boulders. The path widens slightly and enters an area covered with white broom in the spring. At a junction, go right. Pass impressive and distinctive granite outcrops high on the right and come to a granite water **pool**, also on the right.

After a long flat stretch, the path starts to descend again and bears left to become rockier and to descend

The views on the left, to the west, become spectacular.

White broom lines the path that runs alongside the sierra

more steeply. At the bottom of the descent is a T-junction: go right.

Continue along the footpath, which runs almost flat and straight ahead. At one stretch there are bends but keep following the path. Reach a cork oak copse and a Y-junction with a small, overgrown path on the right. Keep left to reach a Y-junction with a dry stone wall ahead and a narrow old metal gate with an arched top set in the middle of the wall. The turning to the left heads for the EX-381 road, which can be seen. Instead take the narrow path to the right.

The path is a bit rocky and ascends slightly with walls and cork oaks on either side. Continue to clear the trees and enter another area of white broom. The path widens at a junction with a track on the left heading for the road. Stay ahead to pass a **farm** and then a vineyard on the right. After the ascent and descent of a small hill, reach a T-junction and go left. Within a few paces turn left again, down another track.

Follow the track as it descends slightly to come to a T-junction, where you turn right. At another junction go left, and a modern white building on the outskirts of the village can be seen ahead. The church tower comes into view ahead and right. At a Y-junction, pass the white building to the left and continue directly ahead down Calle del Campo to return to the church in the square of **Torre de Santa María**.

WALK 17
Torre de Santa María and the mills

Start/Finish	Main square, Torre de Santa María
Distance	10.5km
Ascent/Descent	320m
Time	3½hrs
Terrain	Village streets, lanes, rough tracks, earth footpaths occasionally paved with granite
Max altitude	775m
Map	IGN 730 Montánchez 1:50,000
Refreshments	Bars and cafés in Torre de Santa María and Montánchez
Access	Turn into Torre de Santa María at the sign on the EX-206 Cáceres–Miajadas road
Parking	On the outskirts of Torre de Santa María
Waymarks	White and yellow flashes, signposts
Spring water	One seasonal spring, one year-round spring

This pretty walk ascends from the village on footpaths shaded by deciduous oaks. Walk highlights are the extensive views of the Sierra de Gredos, over 120km away to the north, and those of the Sierra de Guadalupe 70km to the north-east. The descent goes through a small oak wood and passes an area of ruined and restored mills. There is an optional diversion into Montánchez.

From the square in Torre de Santa María, face the church and walk to the right. Ignore the junction directly behind the church and ignore the first left, Calle Arenal. Walk ahead into Calle Asunción. Ignore the blocked junction on the right as well as the tiny street just before a Y-junction, and go right at the junction.

Reach a crossroads and go straight over. The street becomes a rough track and there is a white and yellow waymark on the wall. Walk ahead past small agricultural fincas on either side to reach a T-junction. Go right towards the sierra, and come to a T-junction with a wide

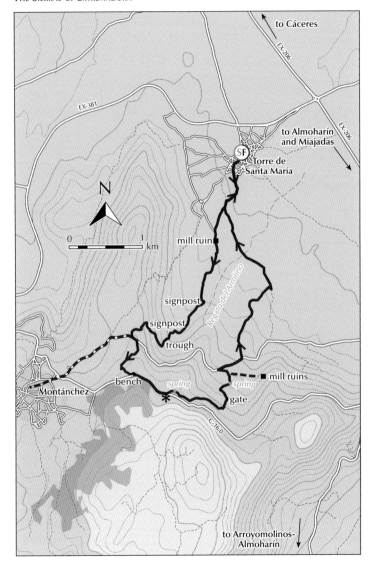

dirt lane. Turn left and reach an open area on the right with a large flat granite rock. Leave the lane and take either of the two tracks on the right; they meet within metres to go up a narrow track which is initially concrete and then earth.

At a wide Y-junction go left. (There is a waymark on the gate post.) Just ahead is the **ruin** of an old mill. Reach a second Y-junction and go right towards the mill ruin. By the ruin is a ford; cross this (in times of high water there are stepping-stones) and ascend gently on the track to reach a Y-junction.

Turn right into a wide footpath of dirt, occasionally paved with granite. At the top of a short climb come to a T-junction with a well-made track, where there are **signposts** with optional walks. Turn right on the track. Ignore small junctions and finca entrances. (There are waymarks at intervals.) At a Y-junction, go left. The track starts to wind and ascend steeply with occasional holm oaks to give shade.

At a wide Y-junction, follow the track around to the right, looking back for great views. Pass a water **trough**

Deciduous oaks line the path before the climb starts in earnest

121

on the right – this dries up in summer but otherwise has drinking water from the spout. Just after the trough the track veers right and ascends even more steeply.

The track becomes a narrow granite-paved footpath and ascends relentlessly. ◄ Reach another set of **signposts** and continue ahead on the footpath, again looking back for the views. Reach a T-junction with a wide lane and turn left, and after a few metres reach a tarmac lane.

The views are extensive on the right.

Detour to Montánchez

At this point there is the option to turn right and follow the road to visit Montánchez and its castle. Reach a roundabout and follow directions from the roundabout in Walk 16. Afterwards, retrace your steps to this point and continue the walk.

At the tarmac lane, even though the waymark indicates not to go left, go left (or straight on if coming from Montánchez). Pass a house on the right and just over the brow of the small hill on the right is a wide track. Take this track, and come to a wide metal gate, which may be open.

Here are lovely views of Montánchez Castle and the Cáceres plains.

Take the footpath to the left of the gate. ◄ It is fairly flat and makes for easy walking. At a Y-junction keep left. Just by a finca where the path curves around to the right is a small building on the left and a junction (waymarked). Turn left: the footpath is rough but the crash barriers of the CC-16.0 can already be seen. Follow the path as it winds past a cork oak grove on the left, and come out on the CC-16.0 and a well-placed **bench** just to the right.

Turn left and walk for 500m on the road. Just after a signposted junction on the right, come to a junction on the left. Turn left and reach a Y-junction at a wide area on the left. Keep right and follow the concrete track as it descends steeply with great **views** ahead and to the right. Pass two granite troughs – the **spring** flowing from the pipe is drinking water.

The track reverts to dirt and reaches a large gate to a house. To the left are two paths: take the one on the right, nearest the house. The footpath is dirt with occasional granite and runs gently downwards with views on the left.

At a T-junction keep right (waymarked). Come to signposts but go straight ahead and reach the start of a deciduous oak wood. On the left is a wide junction; turn left and within 20 paces pass a huge boulder on the right. Within another 50 paces reach a Y-junction where the wider path goes left; turn right onto a narrow dirt footpath with a few granite rocks. After a few more paces turn left on the tiniest of paths and keep straight ahead. Within 20 paces on the left is a dry stone wall, while on the right are boulders and parts of walls. Keep these two walls even on either side.

Dropping down into the small oak wood

Descend for about 100m and reach a dry stone wall across the path. The wall has a gap in it that leads into an enclosure – do not go through the gap. On the right is a small metal **gate**, but turn left and follow the path, keeping the wall on the right. The path is now well-defined and descends through an area of small fincas and oak trees. ▶

Ahead and to the right are the villages of Torre de Santa María and Valdefuentes.

The path bends 90° to the right and becomes wide with compacted earth and lovely views ahead. Descend and pass a **spring** on the right – it is **not** drinking water. Ignore the junction to the right (unless you're going to see

123

Montánchez seen from the castle walls

the mill ruins) and keep on the track to reach a T-junction. Alternatively, follow the waymarks, turning right and walking ahead to visit **mill ruins**. Having done so, return to the T-junction.

Turn left (or go straight ahead if coming from the mill ruins). Reach an unmarked road and turn right to gently descend for a total of 350m. Ignore the first track that goes left and take the second track to the left, which is dirt with occasional concrete and lined with walls. After the last finca entrance the track becomes a soft footpath with a good view of Torre in the distance.

Reach a large, totally flat rock at a Y-junction and go left. At the next Y-junction, also keep left as the path reverts to a track. Reach a T-junction and go right; the track winds to reach another T-junction. Turn left on the wide lane and follow it to the junction where the route initially left the lane. Turn right and retrace your steps back to **Torre de Santa María**.

WALK 18

The oak woods of Zarza de Montánchez

Start/Finish	Stone cross in Zarza de Montánchez on the CC-146
Distance	13km
Ascent/Descent	350m
Time	4hrs
Terrain	Dirt tracks, rough footpaths, partly concrete lane
Max altitude	725m
Map	IGN 730-111 Montánchez 1:25,000
Refreshments	Bars and cafés in Zarza de Montánchez
Access	Take the turning for Zarza de Montánchez from the EX-206 Cacéres–Miajadas road. Arrive at the village but do not enter it. Continue on the CC-146 and reach the parking area.
Parking	Wide lay-by on the CC-146 near the stone cross on the south side of the village
Waymarks	None
Spring water	One well
Linking route	Walk 19

A delightful walk through deciduous oak woods on the north side of Cancho Blanco. From the village, the walk comes to a lake where birds can be spotted almost any time of the year. The track from the lake ascends through cork oak woods and then tiny footpaths climb through dense oak woods; the ascent is steep to reach super views over the countryside to the north, east and south. The descent back to the village is on a track with woods on either side but also passes farming areas. The final stretch is on a hidden narrow path through woods to come back to the village. Take binoculars for views and for watching birds of prey circle overhead.

From the parking area, walk to the **cross**.

> In the 1200s, as the Christians reconquered villages from the Moors, they erected **stone crosses**

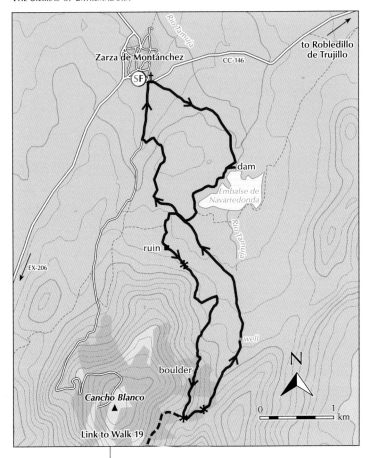

at strategic roads entering the villages. In this way travellers and strangers would know it was a Christian place.

With the village on your left, walk ahead, passing a tarmac lane on the right (which is where the return route rejoins the lane). Within 10m reach a second right turning and take this one to walk on a narrow dirt lane occasionally paved with granite. Stay on the track, ignoring any junctions.

Come to a Y-junction at a well-made stone wall and keep left. Pass over a diagonal crossroads and walk through an area of small olive and fig fincas with areas of pasture. ▸ Ahead, a dam comes into view and a Y-junction offers options of left or right. Go right on the dirt track that ascends to reach a small walkway over the **dam**.

On the right is a copse of deciduous oaks where flocks of azure-winged magpies are often spotted.

The lake, the **Navarredonda**, was constructed in 1997. The river that feeds the reservoir is the Tamuja, which rises in the Cerro San Cristobal and runs northwards for 42km before flowing into the River Almonte. The lake contains drinking water for the village and is a good place to spot birds – especially early and late in the day.

After exploring from the dam return to the dirt track and continue, left, around the lake. Ignore a tempting lane on the right and keep on the track. Come to a

Sunrise over the reservoir

127

Y-junction and leave the track as it continues left around the lake, and take the turning on the right that heads towards the sierra.

Reach a T-junction and turn right. At the next junction, by a sign for low ford, turn left. The track is dirt with a few stones; it is narrow and shaded with oak trees. Stay on this pretty track through a succession of shady cork oak groves, ignoring a junction, right, to continue on the rougher track that ascends gently. Reach an area with two junctions on the right within metres of each other: take the second right.

The track runs parallel to the sierra and become narrower and rougher as it ascends. Pass a **ruin** on the right; further along the track is a stunning **view** over the landscape towards the lake. The track, now a footpath, continues along the side of the sierra with the views all to the left. The path is occasionally encroached by flowering bushes and there are still olive fincas in the area.

Reach a wide Y-junction. The right path is overgrown. Take the left option and follow the path as it descends to reach an open area with another wide Y-junction. Turn right and follow the narrow footpath for the next 1.5km

The route passes old cork oak groves

as it winds its ascent through deciduous oak woods and bushes. There is one Y-junction but keep left on the distinctive path.

At a large, low flat **boulder**, look back for views. Continuing, the path comes out from the woods to give stunning **views** ahead to the south, while on the left is a deep, wooded valley. Reach a T-junction.

Link to Walk 19

For a demanding 26km all-day experience, turn right at the T-junction onto the soft earth footpath to pick up the link with Walk 19. Some 330m to the left of this T-junction, down the concrete track, is where the return rejoins this walk.

From the T-junction, take the concrete track on the left and descend through deciduous oak woods. The steep parts of the track are concrete but the rest is compacted earth. ▶ Pass a **well** with drinking water. The track narrows and passes another well, which is not drinking water.

Pass a junction on the left but keep ahead on the track to pass the junction on the right that goes back to the lake. Continue ahead to retrace your steps for a few metres. Reach the junction on the left, taken earlier, but this time continue ahead.

At a covered well with small granite troughs for animals, turn right onto a dirt track. The narrow track reaches a wide Y-junction, where you turn left. The track becomes a path that runs through shady oak copses and descends between two dry stone walls. ▶ At a Y-junction turn right, and at a T-junction turn right again. Reach a tarmac lane and turn right to walk straight ahead and return to the **stone cross** seen just ahead.

Ahead are views of the Sierras de Alijares (Walk 20) and Santa Cruz (Walk 21). Trujillo can be seen in the middle distance with the Sierra de Gredos beyond.

On the right are pasture and trees while the left has a lovely view down to a wooded valley with fig and olive fincas on the higher sides of the sierra.

WALK 19

Almoharín and the Sierra de San Cristobal

Start/Finish	Plaza de España, Almoharín
Distance	13.5km
Ascent/Descent	590m
Time	5hrs
Terrain	Village streets, dirt lanes, earth footpaths, granite paved paths, rocky tracks, open rough meadows, one short concrete lane, two seasonal streams
Max altitude	825m
Map	IGN 730-111 Montánchez 1:25,000
Refreshments	Bars, cafés and restaurants in Almoharín
Access	By car: Almoharín is on the EX-206 Cáceres to Miajadas road. Access the start from the roundabout at the eastern edge of the village. Turn into the village, pass the park on the left, turn left at El Bulevar and turn right at the mini-roundabout/junction to go all the way up Calle Extremadura to reach the square.
Parking	In the Plaza de España
Waymarks	Cairns
Spring water	One well before the ascent to La Hoya
Linking route	Walk 18
Note	Do not walk with dogs. There may be a few cows grazing the sierra slopes.

This walk leaves the village on a fairly wide, flat lane, through fig and olive fincas. It begins to climb on rockier paths and crosses a meadow to start the sierra climb in earnest. The route follows the valley of La Hoya, a small stream, crosses the valley head and goes flat along a soft footpath to climb up the Cerro San Cristobal before descending back to the village. The walk goes through deciduous oaks, at their most spectacular in late autumn. In spring, flowering bushes are a strong feature on the sierra slopes. There is a high chance of seeing eagles, vultures and smaller birds of prey. There may also be sightings of wild boar, fox and rabbit early or late in the day. The views in all directions are impressive especially from the top of Cerro San Cristobal.

Part of this walk is on a private finca but respectful walkers are welcome. One section of the final descent in on a rocky track that may be slippery if wet.

Starting in the Plaza de España, face the church and walk around it on the left to walk down Calle Real, past a house with a distinctive garden. Take the third junction on the left and walk straight down Calle Santo Domingo, ignoring any junctions. At a big Y-junction with an information board about a local route, go right.

Join a well-made road and turn left. At a Y-junction with a fingerpost pointing right, turn left. Walk on this rough path that occasionally has a stream, **La Hoya**, on the right. Pass a narrow concrete bridge and ford on the right but continue straight on.

Reach the '**Well** of Freedom' on the right. ▸ Just after the well, cross a second concrete **bridge** or ford on the right and take the rough track that ascends. A lane joins the track from the right; continue ahead to pass a ruined barn on the left with almond trees in the garden. Pass a low white farmhouse tucked into a finca on the right.

There is drinking water and a tin can on a string for lifting it.

Just opposite a stone building on the left is a **gateway** on the right. Go through the gateway, leaving the gate as it was found. Walk straight into the finca and then go diagonally to the left on a clearly visible earth footpath parallel to the lane. Walk through two wide gaps in successive walls, pass through a gap in another wall and follow the track as it makes for a stone-built semi-**ruin** visible just ahead – the largest of a few ruins. Pass the building on the left and follow the track straight ahead. Go through a gap in a wall and continue ahead, then slightly left to pick up a clear path that ascends gradually along the side of the sierra. ▸

There are cairns at close intervals to help walkers as this is a much-loved local route.

Occasionally the path runs close to an overgrown lane on the left, distinguishable by parallel walls. The climb becomes steeper as it reaches further into the

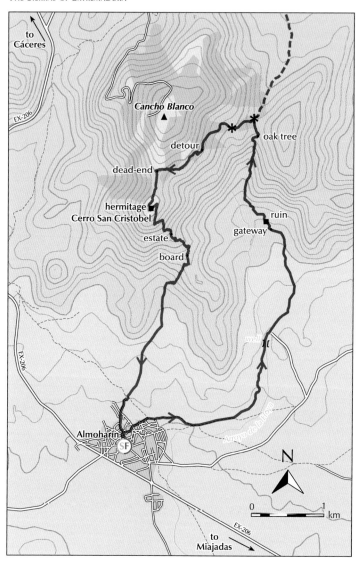

Donkeys are still kept to carry the olive harvest down from the higher fincas

valley. Come to a low wall with two strands of barbed wire on the top; just raise the wire, pass under and step over the wall. The path continues as if the wall does not exist.

The ascent reaches a few small zig-zags. Near the top of the climb the path turns left, follows a wall on the left and bends right, still following the wall. ▶ The path comes very close to the wall on the left as it passes through a gap in a tall hedge and bends to the left.

This is the head of the valley and the views from here are extensive.

The ascent continues, still with the wall on the left, which meets a wall coming down from the right. Turn right at this point to walk up a few metres and cross the wall by a tall deciduous **oak tree** with blue string around it. (The blue string denotes where to cross the wall.) Once over the wall, turn left and enjoy phenomenal **views** all around – especially of the Sierra de Santa Cruz to the north-east. The path comes out onto a concrete lane. ▶

To link to Walk 18, turn right here.

Turn left and ascend for 330m until the concrete ends abruptly at a wide Y-junction. Turn left onto a dirt track; within metres is a sharp Y-junction where you go right onto a narrow earth footpath that goes through an

133

area of deciduous oak trees. (The peak of Cancho Blanco is on the right but the view down on the left is spectacular.) Pass through a small metal gate and cross a seasonal stream using stepping-stones if needed. Cross a wall that has fallen down and then cross a more open area, still following the well-defined path.

Pass through a gap in a wall and pick up another wall on the right. Shadow it, going downhill slightly, then turn right to pass another gap in a wall on the right and ascend. Zig-zag your way through tall retama bushes and come to a wall straight ahead; turn left to pick up the path that goes along the wall, cross through the wall a few metres ahead and follow the path as it ascends. Once through the gap in the wall, come to a T-junction and turn left to ascend in a lane with a wall on either side. ◄

Cerro San Cristobal is just ahead.

As the lane starts to descend, with the hill ahead and slightly left, there is a gap in the wall on the left. Go through this gap to **detour** an overgrown part of the lane. After a few metres, pass a gap and then a second gap. Go through this second gap to return to the lane and the detour ends.

Climb steeply, and just over the high point come to a gap in the wall on the left. Climb through this as the lane terminates in a **dead-end** within a few metres. (There is a gap on the right but ignore it.)

Walk straight across an open space to reach a low hill with scattered rocks and low-growing shrubs. Zig-zag up to find the path and descend the other side of the hill to start the walk up the Cerro San Cristobal. Ahead is a prominent dry stone wall that goes up the hill; make for this wall and once there, walk with it on the right. ◄

The village in the valley to the right is Valdemorales.

The footpath comes to a gap in the wall. Go through and put the wall on your left. Continue up; the path is narrow and winds slightly. Pass a copse of oaks on your left, and at the top come to a flat area of meadow and trees where there are the ruins of the **Hermitage** of San Cristobal.

Keep straight on to cross over a low wall and turn right, enjoying the views all around. Here are the entrance gates to the hermitage and an ancient boundary stone between the villages of Almohárin, Valdemorales and Zarza de Montánchez. Walk straight down from the hermitage gates to find the path within a few metres, and turn left to follow the path until the way ahead is blocked by a wall.

Make a hairpin turn right and follow the path as it gently descends diagonally towards the village, which can be glimpsed ahead. (There are cairns to help guide the way – especially useful when the path makes big zig-zags; to the left, right, left and right again.) There are occasional steep parts to the descent but nothing difficult.

Come out into a meadow behind an impressive collection of ruins of what was once a wealthy family's summer **estate**. Walk to the left of the buildings and come around to the front to pick up the path that goes ahead down shallow, natural steps. Turn left and make a few short zig-zags to follow the path downwards, using the cairns as a guide. The path is now occasionally paved with granite and makes a few twists and turns, bears left and comes to a gap in a wall, followed by another gap in a parallel wall – both of which you should go through.

Valdemorales with the Sierra de Montánchez behind, seen from the summit of the Cerro San Cristobal

Ancient boundary stone between the villages of Almoharín, Valdemorales and Zarza de Montánchez

Enter an open wider area. The two walls just gone through define an overgrown lane; keep these two walls on the right while walking through the open area. Go through a gap in the wall on the right to walk in the lane where it is less overgrown. Go slightly left to leave the wall and pick another one up ahead. Climb over the wall, and just on the left is an information **board** describing the fine view that can be seen from this point.

Now turn right to follow the rough, boulder-strewn track steeply down until the way ahead is blocked by a wall. Turn right and continue downwards on multiple zig-zags, and at the bottom of the descent bear left to walk along a rough track that is almost flat. Come out at a wide compacted earth lane and continue to descend, ignoring all junctions.

Enter the top of **Almoharín** and walk down Calle Santa Filomena, which becomes Calle Hernán Cortés. Reach the back of the church and walk around it to arrive back in the square.

WALK 20

The Sierra de los Alijares

Start/Finish	Plaza de España, Robledillo de Trujillo
Distance	7.5km
Ascent/Descent	300m
Time	3hrs
Terrain	Village streets, rough tracks, earth and granite-paved footpaths
Max altitude	738m
Map	IGN 730 Montánchez 1:50,000
Refreshments	Bars and cafés in Robledillo
Access	By car: from the Cáceres–Miajadas EX-206, turn at the sign for Zarza de Montánchez. Pass that village and keep going on the Carretera de Zarza-Montánchez until you get to the village. Robledillo can also be approached via Trujillo and the village of Ibahernando.
Parking	In the Plaza de España
Waymarks	Patchy posts signed 'Sierra de los Alijares' for part of the way
Spring water	None en route

The start from Robledillo is a gentle climb which then becomes a fairly flat path along the side of the sierra. The wildflowers and flowering bushes are amazing in spring. The middle of the walk has a short, sharp climb giving extensive views towards the Sierra de Santa Cruz (Walk 21). This is followed by a gentle descent through expanses of wild peonies in April and May. The final part of the walk is a steeper descent back to the village flanked by a profusion of flowering bushes in spring. With the flowers come the birds, bees and butterflies. It is a very pretty walk.

Start from the Plaza de España. With the church and the fountain on your left, walk ahead up Calle Gabriel y Galan, and at the wide junction keep right to walk up Calle Extremadura. At the Y-junction with the telephone

Robledillo de Trujillo

box, follow Calle Extremadura as it bears right. Keep going, ignoring all junctions. Once past Calle Manuel Montero on the right there is a Y-junction; take the left turning (the right is where the return will rejoin the street). The street becomes narrower. Bear left and continue past a row of old houses, and at the end of the road, in front of a house numbered 74 and at a Y-junction, turn left to leave the village.

Ascend the concrete lane. Ignore a turning left, and bear right to start up a rough dirt track. Just after a wide, rough space pass an **agricultural building** on the left of the track, which now gets narrower and very rocky. At a Y-junction bear right to walk over some large granite boulders and take a small rough path climbing upwards.

Large, flat boulders pave the path, many of them natural or laid hundreds of years ago.

Come to a wide, open space on the left. The path bears slightly right and continues up. ◀ Ascend steadily through an area dotted with small olive fincas and gates; oak trees grow thinly but there are many flowers underfoot between the granite slabs and rocks and in the verges. Pass a **well** on the right – and take care as there is nothing to stop you falling in.

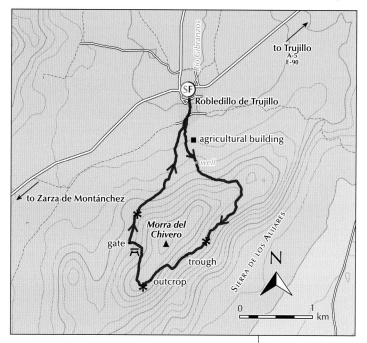

The ascent continues and enters a deciduous oak wood. At the top of the climb the path becomes almost completely flat, narrows and goes through tall swathes of cistus and lavender.

CISTUS

Cistus, part of the rockrose family Cistaceae, is a flowering bush that is wide-spread throughout Extremadura. In fact there are very few walks where cistus does not feature. There are 20 different types of cistus but the most common to this area are the white flowered *Cistus salvifolius* and the pink *Cystus albidus*. The variety of cistus with the brown-red fleck at the base of each white petal, *Cistus ladanifer*, is known as *jara* in Spanish. It is the flower of Extremadura.

There may be birds of prey overhead.

The path runs almost flat in a reasonably straight line along the side of the Sierra de los Alijares. On the left is a considerable drop to the plain below, and on the right is a small range of hills topped by rocky outcrops. ◄ Reach a fabulous **viewpoint**, after which the path enters a copse of oak trees before going up slightly then dropping down to a large open meadow with multiple granite water **troughs**. (These catch flowing water for animals – it is not drinking water.)

The path leaves the meadow on the opposite side of the point of entry. Ahead is a huge and dramatic rocky outcrop, the highest point of the walk. At a small clearing there is a tiny path, left, but ignore this. The path bends 90º to the right and ascends steeply over rocks. At the top of the short climb, veer left; the path narrows and within 20m there is a deciduous oak copse. Descend, then ascend the path to reach the rocky **outcrop** seen earlier. ◄

Look out for peonies, asphodels and orchids, in season, along this path.

Once at the top of the climb, by the rocky outcrop, enjoy the **views**: the mountain behind is the Sierra de Santa Cruz. Once over the peak of the climb, the descent reveals yet more views. Use the walls on either side of the path as a guide, and within 50m the path turns 90º to the right and becomes a wide track.

The view ahead is of the plains to the north-west and the village of Salvatierra de Santiago.

After a few uphill steps there are carpets of peonies and bluebells, in season, and tall deciduous oaks. The track is lined with walls, which are far apart. ◄ As the track descends it narrows to become a path. On the left, the village of Zarza de Montánchez comes into view. Reach a terraced **picnic area** with wooden tables, benches and a barbecue.

The path makes a decisive left turn to go downwards. The descent is sharp with zig-zags and boulders but it is not difficult. Within about 100m the path narrows and is lined with white broom, in season. It comes out at a large open expanse of grass by a metal **gate** in a wall on the left. There is a Y-junction: ignore the left turn and go right.

The path is narrow and passes pretty areas of pasture on the left and tree-covered hills on the right. Behind is a good **view** of Cancho Blanco. The path enters a stretch

Flower-filled meadow and the threat of a late spring downpour

where the trees and bushes encroach and give shade; it narrows and continues downward. Robledillo comes into sight and beyond is a view of the Sierra de Santa Cruz, while in the distance is the Sierra de Gredos.

At a Y-junction, keep left. The path comes out to a large rocky area but continue straight down along a clear, rocky path. At the next Y-junction, keep left again. The path becomes closed-in by trees and, apart from the village ahead, the views are restricted. Ignore a junction right and keep left. At the following junction ignore the left path and bear right, passing gates.

The path passes a huge granite-paved area – take care when it is wet – with a lovely view of the church ahead. It narrows once more, flanked with high hedges, as it comes to the first outbuildings of the village. Go left at the first Y-junction onto a lane, and at the next Y-junction keep right past 'Villa Juan Ruiz 2011'.

The lane bears right. At a T-junction with one of the main roads in the village, turn right and walk all the way down the road without taking any junctions. At a Y-junction, where we went left at the start, join Calle Extremadura to retrace our steps to the starting point in **Robledillo de Trujillo**.

WALK 21
The Sierra de Santa Cruz

Start/Finish	Plaza de España, Santa Cruz de la Sierra
Distance	8.5km
Ascent/Descent	420m
Time	5hrs
Terrain	Village streets, dirt lanes, earth footpaths, granite-paved paths, rocks to climb in a few places, open rough pasture
Max altitude	808m
Maps	IGN 706 Madroñera, IGN 730 Montánchez, IGN 731 Zorita (all at 1:50,000)
Refreshments	Bars and cafés around the square and dotted around Santa Cruz
Access	By car: Santa Cruz de la Sierra is signposted from the A-5 between Trujillo and Miajadas. Turn into the village and go straight along the CCV-241. At a Y-junction go right, straight down Calle Nuflo de Chaves to reach the Plaza de España.
Parking	In the Plaza de España
Waymarks	White and turquoise flashes, cairns
Spring water	Two springs on the way down from the necropolis
Note	Not recommended for vertigo sufferers. Do not walk in the wet – the granite rocks will be slippery.

Although the walk is short, it is strenuous – at one point going up 130m within a distance of 500m. The views are extensive and 360° at the summit: on a clear day the Sierra de Gredos can be seen 100km to the north. The sierra is covered in impressive outcrops of rocks but also has historical reminders of the people who once lived here: a Celtiberian necropolis, a Roman water channel, a Moorish *aljibe* (cistern or small reservoir) and abandoned homes from the last century. Many flowering bushes cover the sierra sides, especially white broom. In spring there are many flowers. Almond trees grow near the summit but the high part of the sierra is not wooded. Birds of prey circle overhead while songbirds inhabit the lower slopes.

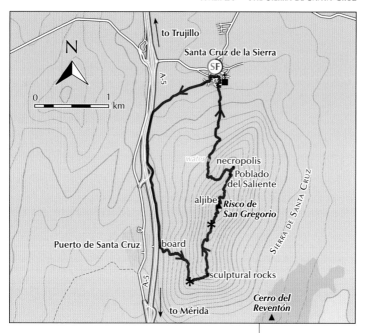

With the church in the Plaza de España on your right, walk straight down Calle Nuflo de Chaves to the left of La Taverna. Ignore the first junction on the left and at the second one turn left into Calle General Sanjurjo. This street bends left, then right. At a multiple junction go second right. At a Y-junction bend left into Calle Burgos and stay on this street.

As the street leaves the village it becomes Calle del Puerto, a wide dirt track. Continue ahead, ignoring junctions, until the track joins another one coming from the right. Turn left and continue on the new track as it runs parallel to the **A-5**, which is over on the right. Pass two junctions on the right which go under the A-5 to the village of Puerto de Santa Cruz.

At a flyover of the A-5 on the right, look left. There is an information **board**, 'Sierra del Puerto'. Just by this

Look out for the white and turquoise waymarks painted on rocks.

board is a small footpath ascending the sierra. It immediately divides: take the left path and go up.

The path is narrow and rocky; it ascends with occasional dry stone walls on either side. ◄ Come to a junction: a level path goes right by an impressive old tree but, turn left to continue up on the rocky path. The path starts with very small zig-zags as it ascends but the waymarks come thick and fast and include small directional signs. If in doubt, go up.

To the north the Sierra de Gredos can be seen on clear days, and on the left are impressive granite outcrops.

After a small level section, which gives time to enjoy the views, the path ascends even more steeply over large rocks to reach a level stretch along the side of the sierra. The **views** over towards Cancho Blanco beyond Puerto de Santa Cruz are especially fine. ◄

Continue on the earth footpath as it passes rocky outcrops on the left to reach an area of **sculptural rocks** shaped over millennia. The path goes to the left of the rocks and continues level. Pass an abandoned house and follow the waymarks to turn left and continue up with immense boulders on the left. Look back at the views – but they are vertigo-inducing so take care!

As the ascent continues, rocky outcrops on the right come into view and the path goes between them, left and right. Near the first summit of the Sierra de Santa Cruz, pass between two large boulders, then continue up. Reach an open grassy area with the top half of a distinctive round boulder on the right: it looks as though the path continues to the left of this boulder, but it doesn't. Pick up the path further left; it is level but then goes up, bends left and goes up some more to reach a rocky outcrop with a rock balanced on the top. The surrounding area is open and grassy with views on both sides of the sierra.

There is a directional waymark on the rock below the balancing rock. Go right to walk along the top of the sierra ridge and look out for more waymarks. The path is clear but rocky in places and descends as well as ascends. In a matter of minutes, reach a wall on the left and follow the path as it hugs the wall. (There are waymarks.)

The path reaches another wall; at this point turn right and pass through a gap in the wall. Another wall appears as a guide, on the left. At one point the path leaves the wall to go right, bypass overgrown vegetation, and then return to hug the wall. Ahead is an outcrop of rocks and the ascent is dotted with almond trees. The final ascent is steep over boulders.

Almond blossoms near the summit

The path comes out to give a 360° **view** that is stunning. Walk slightly left along the sierra ridge to make for the big pile of rocks ahead. Look slightly right at the rocks: there are two, side by side, both with waymarks. From here take the short climb up to the top of the crag, the **Risco de San Gregorio**, where you'll find a Moorish aljibe built to collect rainwater. ▶

This is the highest point of the walk and a great picnic spot with 360° views.

The sierra has been continuously inhabited by different groups of people since pre-Celtiberian times. The area was of strategic importance to the **Moors** as it was situated between Montánchez and Cáceres. Although simple constructions have been discovered dating back millennia, it was the Moors who renovated them and put them to defensive use.

145

Retrace your steps from the aljibe and at the bottom of the twin rocks with the waymarks, turn left, pick up the path and descend. The path bends right around the aljibe rocks and then veers further to the right. It is a little rocky and meanders but descends gradually. Occasionally there are immense sides of rock to cross but these are almost flat. Ahead is a group of rocky outcrops and the path makes for the outcrop on the left, which is made of what looks like hewn boulders. It has a name – the **Poblado del Saliente**. On the right is an information board.

The path continues to the right of the Poblado and descends to an area of level pasture, a few ruined buildings, rocky outcrops and an information board about the **necropolis**. To see the necropolis, walk 100m with the outcrops on your left. The excavations are slight but the depressions of tombs can be seen. Afterwards return to the necropolis information board.

Giant rocks and white broom below the 'Poblado'

This area, now called **Campo Sagrado**, was known to have been a place of religious worship. Scattered around are now-fallen monoliths of granite, which

once formed a circle. Two altars and sacrificial stones were erected within the circle. The remains of tombs can be identified; these were remodelled and reused by the Moors who outlined the tombs with the granite stones that can still be seen.

With the largest rocky outcrop on the right, pick up the granite path going down, indicated by cairns. Pass a board with information about Cancho de la Misa. ▶ Continue the descent until a gap in the wall on the right is reached. (There may be an improvised gate designed to stop motorcycles using the path.) Go through the gap and the path becomes softer with vegetation encroaching. Reach a meadow with three granite troughs and drinking **water** coming from a pipe.

Walk to the left of the troughs and follow the path downwards. Pass a granite water channel once attributed to the Romans but now dated much later. (There is an information board.) Pass through gentle pasture and reach a second trough with drinking water. With the trough on your right, walk its length and drop down to the right.

At a distinctive open space with two dead trees – one with a huge hole in the trunk – follow the path as it bends left and continues the gentle descent. Go through a gap in the wall, marked by magnificent cairns. Come to another metal gate prohibiting motorcycles and go through the gate.

The earth footpath comes out from the sierra, bends left and runs between two stone walls with delightful verges. The village appears ahead. Pass a shepherd's hut on the right, and a small track comes from the right to join the path. Go left on the wider track, which comes to an abandoned **convent** on the right. (The door is always open: go in and explore.)

Retrace your steps to the track, turn right and go down the street, Barrio Santa Rita, as it bends left. Reach a house numbered 14 and turn right. Straight ahead is a small square with a multiple junction; turn left and go ahead to arrive back in the square of **Santa Cruz de la Sierra**.

This is a group of distinctive granite rocks, possibly menhirs, shaped by primitive axes. They are thought to be between 5000 and 4000 years old and related to religious practices.

SIERRA DEL CAMPILLO AND THE SIERRA DE JUNCALDILLA

WALK 22
Garganta de Cuernacabras

Start/Finish	By the bus stop, Campillo de Deleitosa
Distance	13km
Ascent/Descent	490m
Time	5hrs
Terrain	Village streets, one steep rocky assent, tarmac lane, dirt lanes and tracks some with occasional slate rocks, tiny footpaths that need care
Max altitude	648m
Map	IGN 652-IV Campillo de Deleitosa 1:25,000
Refreshments	A few local bars
Access	By car: leave the A-5 at Junction 219 on the south side of the Miravete Tunnel and head on the EX-386 to Deleitosa. From there follow the signs to Campillo de Deleitosa.
Parking	Near the bus stop and children's play park
Waymarks	None
Spring water	Near the start in the small square
Note	Walking poles are useful on two small steep stretches and on tiny footpaths on the side of the sierra.

The initial steep ascent gives way to a long and gentle downhill with stunning views of the jagged, slate-topped Sierra de Juncaldilla. The winding Cuernacabras river is fed by numerous small waterfalls, impressive after the winter rains. The middle part of the walk is a long and almost flat stretch in the water channel that follows the side of the Cuernacabras. Ruins dot the valley and tell of past human activity. The countryside blooms with flowering bushes during the spring: broom, retama, lavender, thyme, rosemary, Spanish heath and cistus. Griffon vultures circle overhead. Take binoculars.

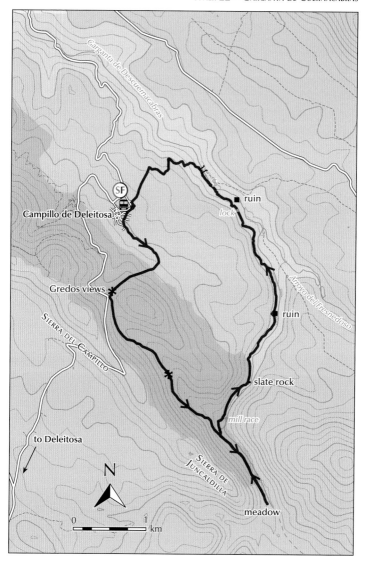

With the bus stop and play park behind, walk to the left of the Correos – the building in front – and up Calle Pilar. Ignore junctions and stay on Calle Pilar. Come to a small square with trees, a pond and drinking water; keep left and walk up Calle Francisco Pizarro. Keep left to leave the village and start on a dirt track, which you stay on as it rises gently. Ignore a junction on the left, and at a Y-junction take the right fork.

Stay on the track as it becomes rough with small slate chips underfoot. Pass through an area of trees to open out into a recently reforested area. The track starts to ascend very steeply – in 700m gain 100m in height. ◄ Ignore junctions left and right, and at the top of the climb there's a tarmac lane ahead. Turn left before the lane to take the wide earth track into a eucalyptus wood.

Look back for a view of the Sierra de Gredos in the distance.

Within a few metres come to a Y-junction and keep right. Stay on this track as it gently descends through the woods with views on the left over the Cuernacabras valley and emerging **views**, ahead and right, of the Sierra de Juncaldilla. As the track descends more sharply, reach the river in an open **meadow** where there is a ruined building, fallen tree trunks and very tall old trees. A lovely picnic spot.

Retrace your steps for approximately 1200m to come to a small junction on the right that is little more than a tiny footpath. (As an additional marker, a huge rock is visible in the river below and right.) Start to descend to the river, going slightly diagonally to the left. At this stage the important thing is to get down without slipping! The descent is only 100m but needs concentration.

Once at the bottom, turn left to pick up a disused water channel and walk inside the two low walls. The river is to the right but the views are ahead, right and especially behind. Reach a magnificent ruined **mill race**.

The **channel** carried water to make hydroelectric power for the villages in the area over 60 years ago. It is long abandoned but the walk continues inside the channel for the next 4km or so until it comes to

The Cuernacabras river, seen from the lock

an end alongside the ruined hydroelectric building by the river.

There is one place, in the channel and just after the mill race, that is overgrown with brambles. Just step out, left, from the channel, walk past the brambles and step back into the channel. There are occasional places where slate slabs have been laid over the low channel walls: either crawl under them or step out from the channel and walk around to step back afterwards.

After passing through a giant split in the **slate rock**, the scenery and views change. The channel stretches into the distance, and at an impressive curve with arches that span a stream there is a **ruin** near the river. The channel ends in a **lock** and the **ruin** of the hydroelectric building can be seen close to the river on the right.

Turn right after the lock and go down, then diagonally left and further down through broom and retama bushes to follow a tiny goat path along the side of the valley. Way ahead, on the river, a small two-arched bridge can be seen. Do not descend too closely to the river but

Ruins of buildings lie across the river

On the hills opposite are several ruins of buildings made of slate and a still-used goat track.

keep straight on the path until a stepping-stone area over a **waterfall** is reached.

After crossing the waterfall, pick up the path as it continues over some slate slabs and close to a low wall before going left and up on the sloping side of the valley. Use a pole on the right to keep steady. ◄

When level with the **bridge**, continue on the path as it turns left and ascends. At a Y-junction go right onto a wider track and continue as the track ascends and makes several pronounced bends, left and right, with a final decisive left into a well-made lane, Calle Eras. Follow the lane back into **Campillo** and turn left at a T-junction, then turn right to arrive back at the play park.

SIERRA DE GUADALUPE

WALK 23
Garciaz and Pico Venero

Start/Finish	Plaza de España, Garciaz
Distance	17.5km
Ascent/Descent	630m
Time	5½hrs
Terrain	Village streets, dirt tracks, woodland tracks, footpaths
Max altitude	1128m
Map	IGN 706 Madroñera 1:50,000
Refreshments	Bars and cafés in Garciaz
Access	By car: from the EX-208 Trujillo to Zorita road, turn off at Conquista de la Sierra and drive straight through the village. Continue for 14km on the CC-23.5 to reach Garciaz. Once at Garciaz, pass the first junction, left. At the second junction, also left, turn left and follow the road, bearing right at a big T-junction, all the way up into the Plaza de España.
Parking	In the Plaza de España, Garciaz
Waymarks	White and yellow flashes (sometimes sparse)
Spring water	None en route
Note	This walk is not suitable on days of intense sun.

Deciduous forests, especially pretty in autumn, provide one of the highlights of this walk. The route starts from the village of Garciaz and ascends on tracks through extensive areas of cistus bushes. The ascent continues but is shaded with pine and chestnut trees, and there are superb views of the Las Villuercas area. The middle part of the walk enters chestnut and oak forests where the tracks and footpaths are almost level. The return is via a reservoir and along a pretty footpath that shadows the side of the sierra before descending to the village. The usual flowering bushes grow in the open spaces and along verges. Vultures, eagles and hawks fly overhead, especially near the reservoir. There may be domestic horses and pigs in the woods, and foxes and rabbits may also be spotted early or late in the day.

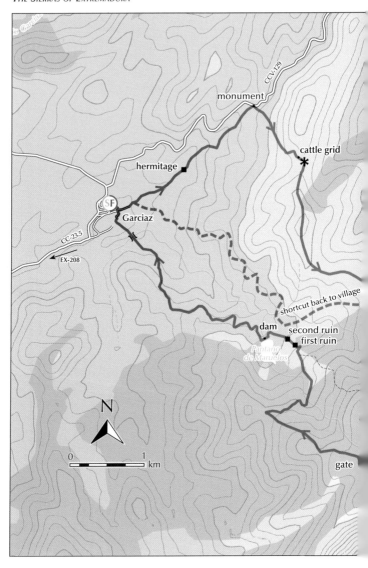

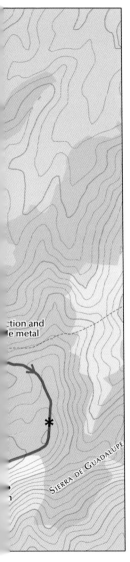

SIERRA DE GUADALUPE

Facing the town hall in the Plaza de España, look left to see Calle los Perales. Walk all the way straight down this street to reach open countryside and views of the sierras ahead. The street becomes a concrete track and crosses over a stream via a low bridge, then the track bears left and gently ascends until it reaches a modern-looking **hermitage** where the concrete stops. Take the track to the left of the hermitage and within 100m reach a Y-junction, then take the small dirt track going sharply up and right. Just ahead, also right, is a pine copse.

The track ascends through extensive areas of cistus bushes. Come to a junction with the CCV-129. On the right, just before the road is a track; take this track. Immediately on the left is a **monument**. ▶

This was erected in 2010 by the Garciaz town hall to commemorate all the workers who have lost their lives in the countryside around the area.

Continue steadily up in the direction of a pine copse on the horizon. There is no shade and the unfolding views on the right are of Garciaz and distant sierras. Cross a **cattle grid** and reach the top of this climb where to the left are stunning **views** of Las Villuercas. Continue on the track around to the right to come to a Y-junction with

155

the pine copse sitting in the middle of the Y. Take the track on the right, then pass a junction on the left but keep ahead. Ignore a track that joins from the left, runs parallel and then disappears left again.

Reach a wide turning on the right – a short-cut back to the village. On the left there is a waymark; go straight on to reach a Y-junction. On the right is a **double metal gate** that is locked. There is a waymark: take the right track as it ascends and enters a deciduous oak wood.

Come to an area where the trees on the left start to thin and there are good views of Las Villuercas. Cross a cattle grid and come to a set of double metal gates with a private property sign. Just to the right of the gates is a small footpath: take this, right. On the left is a waymark on a post and within metres there is a low metal barrier to stop vehicles entering the woods. On the barrier is a waymark and an indicator to turn right. Just after the barrier is a wide Y-junction.

Take the left track – the right goes through the woods and misses Pico Venero altogether – and continue on a track with woods on the right and open **views** to Las Villuercas on the left. Climb gently but steadily to reach the highest point of the walk, **Pico Venero**, at the geodesic marker.

The Instituto Geografía National (IGN) has erected small **geodesic markers** throughout Spain, usually on peaks. These markers are used to measure distances between two points, to enable calculations to be made by triangulation and to collect other geographic data.

The **views** are extensive. Follow the track as it bears right down a magnificent sweep through the woods, and reach a green metal **gate** on the left with a choice of going ahead or taking a track on the right, directly opposite the gate. Go right.

Ignore a path that joins the track from the right and behind. Bear left to continue on the track that descends gently with pine trees on the left. Reach an open area

with a crossroads and turn right. Reach a Y-junction and turn right again. Reach a point where there are white and yellow crosses on both sides of the track. Stop here: do not go ahead. Look right and slightly behind to find a path that bears right, and take that path.

Within 50m reach a second low metal barrier across the path: step over and continue ahead through a densely planted chestnut wood. At an inverted Y-junction stay ahead and do not go left. Come out from the trees as the path bends to the left. (In season there may be water on the path but there are stepping-stones.) Enter an oak wood and reach a private finca with gates on the right. Keep on the path, which bends left.

Come to an open area with views ahead of two red-roofed buildings in a state of disrepair. Garciaz can be seen above the roof of the nearest ruin. Ignore the track that goes right and up, and continue on the path as it descends towards the buildings. ▶ Reach an inverted Y-junction and turn acutely left. (The channel of water crosses under this path as well, but flows from left to right.)

A wide track through the chestnut woods in autumn

In season there is a small channel of water that crosses under the path from right to left.

157

Walk straight ahead through metal gateposts each with a waymark. The path goes up towards the **first ruin**, but turn right onto a small path that heads towards the **second ruin**. Walk through the meadow and pass the ruin to continue ahead through an area of head-high cistus bushes.

The path becomes rougher. At several small buildings the path reaches a wider track that comes from left to right; join the track and go right. Walk through two metal gateposts with a lovely view of Garciaz ahead. Reach a crossroads and turn left to reach the **reservoir**, Pantano de Maruelos, and a picnic area.

Walk to the **dam** over the reservoir and turn right to walk across the dam. Turn right and descend steeply on a rough track, and at the bottom ascend the track ahead. It winds around the side of the sierra and goes in and out of copses, giving views on the right. Reach two metal gateposts that have waymarks: go through to continue ahead.

Reach a T-junction and turn right. At the bottom of a small rough descent the track makes a decisive bend to the left; on the right is a path with two metal gates

Verges filled with spring flowers outside Garciaz

opposite each other (waymarked). Turn right to follow this path and reach a T-junction by a metal gate, then turn left onto a wider track. The village is now visible. Reach a few outbuildings and, ignoring junctions, follow the track, passing over an old **bridge**.

The ascent to the village is on concrete and then tarmac. Once in **Garciaz** proper, keep to the tarmac lane and do not take junctions. Bend right, reach the church and follow it around to the right into Calle Cruz. Keep the church on your left then turn right down Calle Cruz Verde and turn left. The square is directly ahead.

Views of the Sierra de Guadalupe and Las Villuercas on the long climb from the village

WALK 24

Cabañas del Castillo to Navezuelas

Start	Bus stop, Cabañas del Castillo
Finish	Navezuelas
Distance	12.5km
Ascent	720m
Descent	560m
Time	4hrs (plus exploring time)
Terrain	Village streets, small back roads, wide tracks and narrow earth footpaths, one small river with a bridge and two streams with stepping-stones
Max altitude	1042m
Map	IGN 681 Castañar de Ibor 1:50,000
Refreshments	Limited in Cabañas del Castillo but bars and cafés in Navezuelas
Access	By car: for Cabañas del Castillo via the A-5, take the EX-386 direction Deleitosa, then CC-22.2 and CC-22.4. For Navezuelas via the EX-102 to Cañamero, then CC-21.1.1 and CC-97.
Parking	In the open space near the bus stop in Cabañas del Castillo. Alongside the main road, Avda de Extremadura, in Navezuelas
Waymarks	White and yellow flashes (PR CC-144), white and red flashes (GR 117)
Spring water	None en route
Linking route	Walk 25
Note	The route requires a driver or carefully planned buses or a taxi to get back to the start – or park in Navezuelas and get a taxi to the start.

This linear walk is part of the PR CC-144 and the longer GR 117. It begins with a steep climb to the ruined castle for an extensive view of the region's sierras and their parallel valleys. It continues along the side of the Sierra de Alcornocal and descends to cross the wooded valley of the Garganta de Santa Lucía. The ascent from the valley crosses the Sierra de la Ortijuela, and then descends to reach Navezuelas. Pass through oak and cork oak woods, olive groves and chestnut plantations. Cross open ground with low-growing flowering bushes – especially Spanish heath and cistus. Watch for vultures, eagles, hawks and songbirds. There is an optional 1km diversion to visit a natural cave.

Start by the bus stop in Cabañas del Castillo and follow the fingerposts, 'Castillo PR CC-144', up to the castle along Calle de la Peña Buitrera. Ascend the steps and walk past and around the old church, keeping it on the left. Continue up the steep narrow path to the top of the rocky outcrop for the **castle**, originally constructed by the Moors, and the views.

Retrace your steps to pass the church. Take the lane, first left, and walk ahead, then join another lane but keep left. At a clear Y-junction with multiple signs, go right for the PR CC-144.

Walk ahead on this narrow earth footpath through a shady cork oak wood. Pass a high rocky outcrop, **Peña Buitrera**, on the left where vultures nest. Arrive at a Y-junction with a wide track and go left. The track ascends

Peña Buitrera from the Collado de los Zahurdones

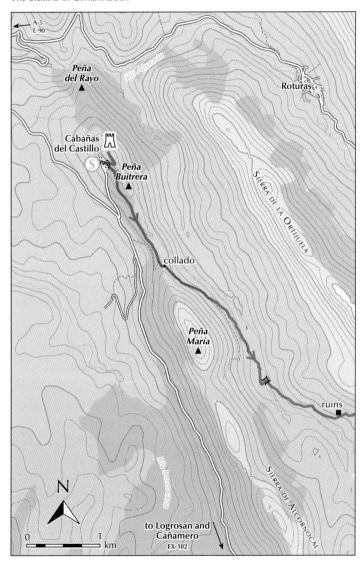

gradually, reaches a bend to the left and arrives at **Collado** de los Zahurdones and the first of many viewpoints. ▷

Descend the main track to come to a crossroads. Keep ahead and left – which is only a continuation of the track. (There is a signpost.) As the track descends, views into the deep valley of the Garganta de Santa Lucía appear below the peaks on the left. At the bottom of the valley cross the river on an old **bridge**.

Continue on the track as it ascends from the valley with views on the right of the Sierra del Alcornocal and the valley of the river crossed earlier. The track passes through olive groves on the left and comes to an abandoned smallholding with **ruins** on either side. Reach a T-junction with multiple signs; here the PR CC-144 meets the GR 117 and the white and red waymarks start. Navezuelas is 8.5km away.

Turn right onto a track reserved for walkers and continue upwards. Reach a shaded area where there are madroño trees, then pass through a cork oak wood where there are glimpses of the Embalse de Santa Lucía on the right – the reservoir fed by the river.

> **Madroño** is the Spanish name for *Arbutus unedo*, also known in English as the strawberry tree. It is an evergreen and has attractive white flowers in the autumn at the same time as the round, red fruits

Peña Buitrera is to the left and the Sierra de la Ortijuela is ahead.

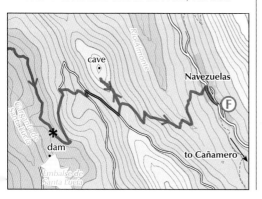

mature. The fruits can be eaten, but take care: local folklore says that too many fruits induce a feeling of intoxication.

The track bends very sharply to the left and the going is uphill into the Sierra de la Ortijuela. A small track joins from behind and right; continue ascending through a cork oak wood to reach a triangular junction. Ignore the left track. The track on the right is the continuation, but look more sharply right: there is a small footpath going through the trees with a low stone wall to its right and red, black and white waymarks. Take this path through head-height flowering bushes and shady trees. The path becomes strenuous as it goes up steeply through the first of the chestnut trees.

Reach a T-junction with a well-made lane and go left. Follow the lane as it bends in a sweep around to the right and continue on the lane as it goes gently upwards, giving **views** on the right over the Embalse de Santa Lucía and the Sierra del Alcornocal. Come to a signpost on the left and go left up the small track. At the top of the short climb reach an open space with a view of Navezuelas on the right.

Detour to the natural cave
To visit a cave, turn left and follow the footpath through a meadow with chestnut trees. Ahead and left are several rocky outcrops; make for the largest one that is the furthest away by following the rough path along the side of the hill and continuing through an area of low-growing bushes. The cave entrance is approached by gently sloping rocks – do not attempt in the wet. Explore the cave, which is not deep but interesting, especially the natural chimney at the back. Retrace your steps to the track beyond the meadow with chestnut trees and turn left to continue.

Descend through chestnut trees with views of the Sierra de las Villuercas and the village on the left. Come to a T-junction, turn left and continue steeply downwards as the track hairpins to the right. At a Y-junction leave the

track to go left over a low wall onto a path that descends steeply, and follow the path through a wood and chestnut plantations, keeping a small fence to the left.

Where the path bends noticeably to the right there is a tiny rough path going off to the left, with a faded waymark on a rock. Take this path, which descends with the sound of running water to the right. Cross a small stream, continue to descend, then cross a bigger stream at the bottom of the descent. Turn left to begin the ascent to the village.

Just before a gateway, ahead, look right to see a white and red waymark. Take the small path, right, to climb steeply up. At a T-junction turn right to make the final ascent and after a left bend reach the **Navezuelas**. Go across the road, walk up between the houses and reach Avenida de Extremadura and a selection of bars and cafés both left and right.

To extend the walk considerably by continuing to **Guadalupe** (Walk 25), turn right at the Avenida de Extremadura and walk 500m to reach a Y-junction. Keep left and on the left is the Co-operativa and the start of Walk 25.

The rock complex containing the cave near Navezuelas

WALK 25
Navezuelas to Guadalupe

Start	Avenida de Extremadura, Navezuelas
Finish	Plaza de Santa María, Guadalupe
Distance	15km
Ascent	650m
Descent	910m
Time	5hrs
Terrain	Village streets, earth footpaths, rocky paths, tracks with occasional granite slabs, woodland tracks, one stream
Max altitude	1230m
Map	IGN 681 Castañar de Ibor 1:50,000 and IGN 707 Logrosán 1:50,000
Refreshments	Bars and cafés in Navezuelas. Extensive options in Guadalupe.
Access	By car: come into Navezuelas on the CC-21.1.1 and then the CC-97, signposted from Cañamero. However, it is better to park in Guadalupe and get the bus to Navezuelas.
Parking	Avenida de Extremadura, Navezuelas (on the right-hand side just after entering the village near the information board). In Guadalupe use the car park on the left of the Carretera de Guadalupe as it bends to the right after the bus park, also on the right.
Waymarks	White and yellow flashes, white and red flashes, GR 117 posts
Spring water	None en route
Linking route	Walk 24
Note	Do not walk on days of poor visibility. The route will need a driver or carefully planned buses or a taxi to get to, or back to, the start.

Part of the GR 117, this is an impressive walk in the high sierras of the region. The initial part of the walk ascends to reach the highest point within the first hour, the path going through chestnut woods and oak trees with a profusion of low-growing flowering bushes – especially cistus and Spanish heath. The rocky path follows the line of the sierra and descends to cross a stream before climbing parallel to the Sierra de las Acebadillas through low-growing flowering bushes and trees to reach a second high point. Thereafter the walk descends and goes through woods of deciduous oak, chestnut and pine. A small stretch on a minor road leads to the last part of the walk, which follows an earth footpath to Guadalupe.

Walk as if to leave the village, passing the Co-operativa del Campo de las Villuercas on the left. ▶ Just after this, take the concrete road in the direction of Guadalupe, which goes up and bends left. Do not bend left again but take the small rough track, right, and climb up between cherry orchards.

Walkers joining from Walk 24 start here.

Follow the track as it ascends very steeply. The track makes a 90° bend to the right and continues up. Pass through a small metal gate on the left, enter a lane, and turn left then right into a chestnut wood. Just at the entrance to the wood there is a sign for Guadalupe and an indication that this is the start of the old hunting route of Alfonso XI.

Take this rough, narrow footpath as it ascends through the woods making occasional hairpin bends and thus shifting the side on which the views appear. Within an hour the path comes out from the trees and arrives at the highest point of the walk – the **Collado** de la Pariera, which is measured at 1240m but is really 10m lower. ▶

The views to the left are extensive, and on clear days the Sierra de Gredos can be seen to the north.

The rocky footpath continues, level along the ridge of the sierra, with views on the left and flowering bushes on either side. The path enters a deciduous oak wood and passes through areas of old rockfalls. There is a white and yellow waymark on a rock – the first on the route. Come to a signpost on the left, 'Collado de los Ajos 1220m'; after this point the path gets wider, rougher and starts to descend with pronounced zig-zags at steeper points.

Come to another **rockfall**. The rocky path zig-zags through it but then becomes soft earth as it goes ahead into another wood of old oaks covered in lichens. In

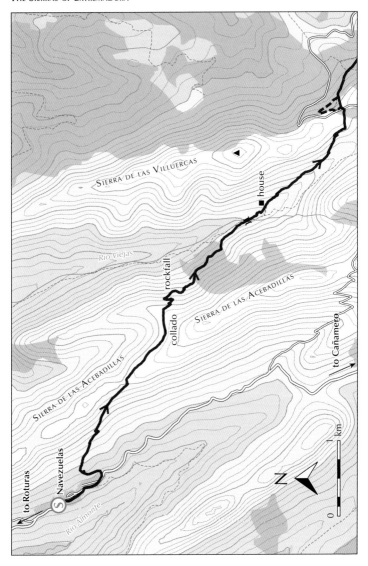

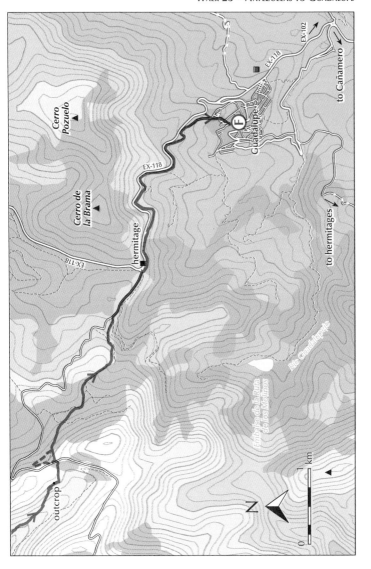

season, a small stream joins the path from the right and follows it for a few metres before disappearing. As the path drops further down, a dirt track can be seen below on the left. The path continues and joins the track, turning right onto it. Keep right.

Within a few metres there is a small path on the left: take this and follow it as it descends to the small Viejas river. The path continues ahead but turn left and cross the river on a small **bridge**. Once over the bridge the path bears right and winds upwards through the woods, then bends right to follow the river, which is on the right. Pass a GR 117 post on the left and come to a small stone-built weekend **house** on the left. Continue upwards with views of deciduous trees, bordering the river, right.

Reach a Y-junction and take the small path that ascends on the left. (There is a GR 117 signpost to help locate the path.) Follow this path, granite-paved, rocky in places, lined by bushes and trees, as it ascends

The path to the granite outcrop

relentlessly to give lovely views of the Sierra de las Acebadillas on the right.

As the path becomes steeper there are zig-zags until an open area is reached with an **outcrop** of giant boulders on the right. The path bends, naturally, around to the left and continues upwards, but much less steeply, to reach a tarmac road, from where there are two possibilities for the initial descent.

Easier option

This option is less steep and easier to negotiate for some. It is 150m longer than the main route. Cross the road and go very slightly left, then cross the top of the steep descent to take the winding path through woodlands and come out opposite a track going into the oak wood, signed GR 117.

To follow the main route, which descends steeply, cross the road with a GR 117 signpost on the right and another saying 'Navezuelas 7.8km Guadalupe 7.1km'. Go very slightly left to start the wide, steep descent on the right, taking care. Halfway down, on the right, is a track going into an oak wood, signed GR 117. ▶

The track goes through the woods and is easy to follow. Come to a crossroads with a very wide dirt lane and go straight over. At both ends of the track is a directional signpost with a red and white waymark on a rock on the right. About 100m later come to a Y-junction with a small path on the left and a GR 117 sign. Take this path.

Come to a wide area, open on both sides, and continue straight over on the path that naturally bends left. (There is a waymark on a rock.) Do not join a wider track on the right but stay on the path as it goes along the edge of the open area, then re-enter the woods on the right. (There is a waymark on a tree to the left.) The path now enters a deep pine wood with abundant Spanish heath.

At the next crossroads go straight over with waymarks to help. Pass a GR 117 post on the left. ▶ Come to a third crossroads with a well-made track and go slightly left, then straight on. The path becomes a wide track and descends straight through the pine wood.

The alternative route rejoins the main route here.

Ahead and right is a good view of Guadalupe.

Garden at the centre of the monastery cloisters

Reach fences on both sides of the path, leading to an unlocked gate. Go through the gate and join a well-made lane and turn right. Follow the lane until a big roundabout is reached where the lane joins the EX-118 Ctra de Navalmoral. On the left is a set of maps showing routes in the area. The 15th-century **Hermitage** del Humilliadero is across the roundabout and to the left.

On the right is a small open space with a set of signposts and a footpath going left. Take this path – do not go right where the path is signed with a cross. The path shadows the road and the valley down into **Guadalupe**. Follow Calle Matoral, which leads into Calle Caño de Abajo and bends right to become Calle Real. Turn left into Calle Nueva de los Capellanes and reach the Plaza de Santa María in front of the monastery.

SIERRA DE LA PELA

WALK 26
Orellana de la Sierra

Start/Finish	Plaza de Garcia de Bejarano, Orellana de la Sierra
Distance	7.5km
Ascent/Descent	340m
Time	2½hrs
Terrain	Village streets, concrete lanes, rough tracks, granite-paved and earth footpaths, one rocky ascent and descent
Max altitude	635m
Maps	IGN 754 Madrigalejo 1:50,000 and IGN 755 Navalvillar de la Pela 1:50,000
Refreshments	A few bars and cafés in Orellana
Access	By car: come into Orellana de la Sierra via Orellana la Vieja and signs for the EX-115 and Navalvillar de Pela. At the sign for Orellana de la Sierra turn into the village at the main junction and Calle Tejar. Turn right at Calle Nueva, then third left down Calle Consejo which becomes Calle Cristo. Pass the Plaza de Garcia de Bejarano on the left and park.
Parking	Plaza de Garcia de Bejarano
Waymarks	None
Spring water	None en route
Note	Not suitable on days of intense sun.

This short walk climbs out from the village through olive groves and ascends onto the lower slopes of the Sierra de la Pela. A short ascent through a pine wood comes to a narrow footpath which runs along the side of the sierra. Views of the Orellana reservoir and of Orellana la Vieja on the Guadiana river are constant on this part of the walk. The path is lined with hundreds of flowering bushes and wildflowers. Occasional evergreen oaks and wild olives grow here but it is the juniper bushes that dominate. Birds of prey fly overhead; this walk is in a Protection Area for birds.

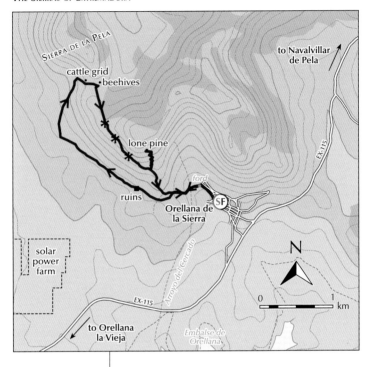

With the Plaza de Garcia de Bejarano and the Palace on your left, walk down Calle Cristo, going away from the village. The street ascends then descends to leave the village. Turn left to cross a small **ford** over a stream and follow the concrete lane up to reach a Y-junction. Turn left onto a dirt track. ◄ Ignore all junctions into fincas and keep on the dirt track, lined with olive groves, as it passes some agricultural **ruins**. As the track ascends and descends, on the left are views of a huge solar power plant.

Look back for views of the village and left to see glimpses of the lake. On the right is the sierra.

Come to a T-junction and turn right towards the sierra. The track ascends and bends slightly right while narrowing. Reach a Y-junction where the main track bends left; take the much narrower track, now a path, that goes up on the right. It becomes rougher and steeper as it climbs into the sierra.

At what looks like a Y-junction, the left turning goes into a finca while the right bends decisively to the right. Go right, and at another entrance to a finca on the right, the path bends left and continues the ascent. Reach the top of the climb and a **cattle grid**; cross the grid and enter an open area surrounded by pine trees.

Look around. On the left, behind a fenced area with a gate, are seasonal **beehives**. The path continues ahead into the pine wood, but do not go that way. Look back at the cattle grid: on the left is a small fence. Turn left to negotiate a few large boulders and walk ahead with the fence on the right to reach a broad track ascending through the pine wood. Take this track, which soon narrows.

At the top of the first climb the track bends right, then left, to reach an area with low-growing flowering bushes where the track bends left. Look right: there is a small granite-paved footpath going through dense cistus bushes. Take this path.

The defined path runs along the side of the sierra without junctions. It is reasonably flat but occasionally

Solar power plant seen from the top of the climb

View south from the lone pine

Look out for birds overhead.

rough with encroaching bushes – especially cistus, lavender and juniper. However, it is never overgrown. The **views** are ahead and right and there are many vantage points and one especially fine **viewpoint**. ◄

Reach a huge wall of natural rock on the left with tremendous open **views** of the lake and Orellana la Vieja ahead. The path starts a gentle descent after this point and is flanked with olive groves.

Come to a large rock fall on the left; high up and slightly left is a magnificent **lone pine tree** from which a panoramic view can be seen. To make the small detour, leave the path, turn left and ascend the stony zig-zag path up to the tree. After enjoying the views retrace your steps back to the original path, turn left and continue the gentle descent.

Three unsightly masts come into view. Reach a T-junction, turn left and continue to walk between the communications masts. The path now becomes a concrete track and descends towards the village below. Reach the junction near the village and turn left onto the concreted lane to retrace your steps over the ford and turn right back to the starting point in **Orellana de la Sierra**.

THE SOUTHERN SIERRAS

The Sierra de Aguafría (Walk 32)

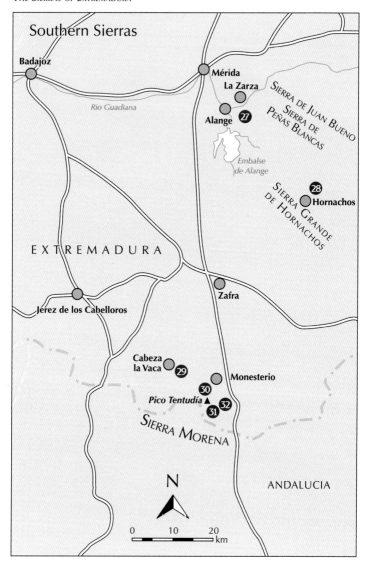

SIERRA DE PEÑAS BLANCAS
AND SIERRA DE JUAN BUENO

WALK 27
La Zarza

Start/Finish	Plaza de España, La Zarza
Distance	17.5km; shorter route: 7.5km
Ascent/Descent	550m; shorter route: 340m
Time	5hrs; shorter route: 2½hrs
Terrain	Village streets, dirt tracks, stony tracks, earth footpaths – occasionally paved with granite slabs
Max altitude	500m
Map	IGN 803 Almendralejo 1:50,000
Refreshments	Bars, cafés and restaurants in La Zarza
Access	By car: La Zarza lies just off the EX-105 north of Alange. Follow the directions for 'centro urbano' after turning into the village.
Parking	Park just before reaching the Plaza de España where the street is wide enough for nose-to-kerb parking
Waymarks	Signposts, white and red flashes
Spring water	None en route

The Sierras of Peñas Blancas and Juan Bueno are very different. The first is rugged and covered in flowering bushes with copses of holm oaks. The route climbs up steeply from a stream bed outside the village and a footpath leads to paintings on a cave wall dating from between 5000BC and 2000BC. The pretty stretch along the sierra ridge gives magnificent views over Alange reservoir. The joining route between the sierras is through olive groves, and then the second sierra is lower and softer. It is mainly planted with eucalyptus and flowering bushes, with views of farming countryside to the north.

The walk can be cut short after the first sierra. Take binoculars for the views and the birdlife.

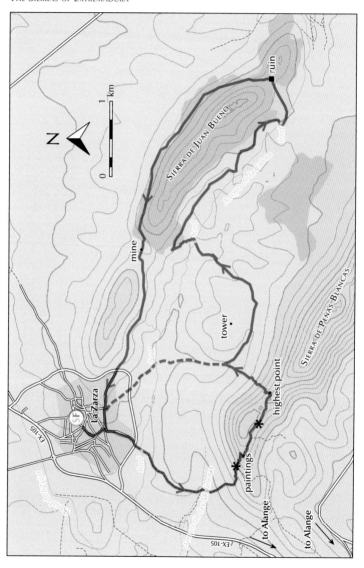

Start in the Plaza de España at the corner with Calle el Pilar and outside Bar Saturio. Walk straight up Calle el Pilar to reach a roundabout with a low hedge around the centre. Keep to the left on the roundabout and take the second left exit into Calle el Pozo. Follow this street up to a time and temperature clock in the centre of the street where there is a crossroads. Go right at the waymark, and at the next junction, a few metres away, go left as indicated.

Come to a junction and go straight ahead. Waymarks are plentiful and painted on almost everything possible. Come to a crossroads and go ahead again, and at the adjoining Y-junction go right. Reach the end of the village where the street turns into a rough track: ahead is a view of the entire Sierra de Peñas Blancas with the Castillo del Culebra on its hill to the right.

The **Castillo del Culebra** dates back to the ninth century and Moorish times. It was captured by the Christians during the Reconquest in the 13th century but abandoned 300 years later. *Culebra* is the Spanish word for snake. The castle gets its name not

The overhanging cave wall on which the paintings can be found

181

from an association with snakes but because the approach snakes up the hillside.

Follow the track down to reach the village ring road. On the left is a signpost for 'Pinturas Repuestres La Calderita'. Go straight over the road where the track continues to descend to a small stream, the Arroyo de la Calera, by a **ford** with stepping-stones. Continue ahead on the track; the going is uphill between olive fincas and there are almond trees lining the track.

The village of Alange comes into sight as the track continues to ascend and becomes stonier. ◀ Descend past agricultural buildings on the right and reach a Y-junction. Go straight ahead, ignoring junctions. Follow the waymarks as the track narrows considerably to become a footpath with the sierra looming ahead and left. The railings that protect the site of the cave paintings can be seen high on the left.

The path bends left, giving extensive **views** of La Zarza and the countryside. As it ascends it draws nearer the base of the sierra and the rocks become numerous. A zig-zag aids the ascent to a signpost; 'La Zarza

To the right and below the castle is the dam that controls the town's reservoir.

Along the sierra ridge with Alange below

182

3km, Puerto de las Hoyos 1km, Pinturas Rupestres La Calderita'.

To reach the **cave paintings**, turn right on the narrow path and ascend, then descend the few metres to the cave. ▸ After visiting the paintings, retrace your steps to just above and behind the signpost and take the path on the right to rejoin the main path.

Turn right and continue the steep ascent through a more open area where there are numerous paths but all reaching the top. Once at the top, look left to see a waymark indicating the start of the path along the top of the sierra. Before taking it, enjoy the view of Alange and its reservoir. To the right of Alange is the Sierra de Hornachos (Walk 28), and on the right is the city of Mérida. Look up for birds of prey.

The paintings are slight but important evidence of human activity in the area 4–7,000 years ago.

ALANGE

Alange is a Roman spa town, very popular during the time when Mérida was the capital of Lusitania, Rome's most westerly province. Then it was known as Aquae. Every minute, 216 litres of water, at a steady 28°C, flows into the baths originally built during the time of Flavius. Although the baths fell into disuse during medieval times, Alange is now once again a flourishing spa resort.

Pick up the waymark to start the path along the sierra. The going meanders up and down, occasionally stony, but always with a view. Reach a signpost at the Puerta de las Hoyos, the **highest point** of the walk. From here the path descends slightly.

Come to a waymark indicating left and downwards. There are paths that continue along the sierra to the right but this walk goes left at this point. Descend carefully as the path is steep and rough in places. Follow the waymarks, which are plentiful, and do not cross over the low boulders cutting off other paths. Reach a definite Y-junction, turn right and within a few metres reach a T-junction. Turn left to continue the descent through trees. Cross a ford and come to a T-junction.

Short-cut back to La Zarza

For a shorter walk (7.5km) back to the village, turn left. The return is along a wide rough track that descends, crosses a **ford**, bears left and ascends to reach the village ring road. Cross the road to reach **La Zarza** and follow the instructions near the end of this walk to return to the start.

For the continuation of the walk, turn right. (There is a yellow arrow on a rock.) The track is stony but lined with flowering bushes, especially cistus, and the Sierra de Peñas Blancas is to the right. At a Y-junction go left; on the left is a modern house with a circular tower with a metal staircase winding around it.

Pass a small house with an imposing gateway on the left, then reach a crossroads and go straight ahead. The track bends to face the Sierra de Juan Bueno and becomes stonier. Come to a second crossroads with the **Arroyo de la Calera** just ahead; the waymark indicates right but continue straight ahead and cross the stream at the ford.

Reach a Y-junction and turn left, then at a junction turn sharp right to pick up a well-made track that runs flat, more-or-less straight, and parallel to the sierra on the left. Reach a junction, ignore the option left, and of the two options on the right take the second one.

Reach another junction and ignore the track that goes right and downhill. Instead keep left, which continues ahead into a eucalyptus wood. The track reaches a utility pole on the left where there is a Y-junction. Go left; on the left is a large house and ahead is a modern house. Pass between a second utility pole and the gates to the house on the left, and come to a T-junction with two options on the right and one on the left. There is another house just ahead. Take the second right option in the direction of a white farmhouse and a third utility pole on the right.

The track passes through eucalyptus wood with densely growing flowering bushes. As it comes out from the wood there is a Y-junction: take the left turning (waymarked). ◄ Ignore a junction left and walk ahead

Waymarks continue for the rest of the walk.

where there is a utility pole on the left and an impressive **ruin**, the Casa de Don Andrés, ahead and right.

The track makes a decisive bend to the left. On the right is a signpost; go right, then keep on the straight track all the way to a limestone mine, ignoring any junction. The eucalyptus wood is on the left but there are glimpses of the agricultural plains between the thinner trees on the right. There is an abundance of flowers in the spring, including orchids. The **mine** comes into view and the track drops down at this point. There is a signpost on the left with an information board in Spanish.

> The **Tierrablanca (white earth) Mine** was started over 100 years ago and was a huge employer. The mineral mined here is limestone. Heated, it provides lime traditionally used to paint the outside of houses white to reflect the sun. The men who sold the product from panniers on donkeys were a familiar sight in southern Spain. The mine is still operational but only employs a few people. Lime is still popular as it allows damp walls to 'breathe'.

The village is now 3.1km away. The track drops down more steeply to reach a wide junction; go left to ascend between two water-filled pits. At the top of the small climb, keep left. The track becomes wider. Ignore junctions because the track goes straight back to the village.

At a Y-junction with an agricultural building on the left, follow the waymark to go left. The village and the church tower come into view as the track meets the village ring road. Cross over the road. ▸

The short-cut rejoins the main route here.

Walk straight down Calle la Mina. At the Y-junction go left to stay in Calle la Mina. Come to Calle Buenavista and turn right, then go left down Calle Pila de los Frailes. At the end of this street turn right and right again, then first left into Calle Pozo. Reach the square. Pass the central roundabout to the right to reach Calle el Pilar, at the end of which is the bar, the Plaza de España and the car parking area in **La Zarza**.

SIERRA GRANDE DE HORNACHOS

WALK 28

Hornachos

Start/Finish	Bus stop outside La Parada restaurant, Hornachos
Distance	14km
Ascent/Descent	670m
Time	5hrs
Terrain	Village streets, cobbled lanes, dirt tracks, earth and rocky paths
Max altitude	778m
Map	IGN 830-III Hornachos 1:25,000
Refreshments	Bars, cafés and restaurants in Hornachos
Access	By car: reach Hornachos via Mérida, Almendralejo, Villafranca de los Barros and Ribera del Fresno. Enter Hornachos on the EX-342 and keep straight on the EX-343 and EX-344 for La Parada.
Parking	In the streets and side streets around the La Parada triangle
Waymarks	Sporadic and various: lilac, yellow, but none related specifically to this route
Spring water	None en route
Note	To visit the Moors interpretation centre, ask at the tourist office before starting the walk.

This super walk, with good viewpoints from the sierra summits, crosses over the Sierra Grande de Hornachos twice and takes in a visit to the ruins of Castillo Mora on its rocky hill outside the village. The sierra is a designated area of special conservation. It is covered in cistus, lavender, rosemary and Spanish heath flowering bushes. There are holm and cork oak woods, juniper trees and many species of lichen – especially the silvery fruticose variety. For bird lovers there are plenty of songbirds in the air and raptors riding the thermals above the higher peaks. The Sierra Grande is a Protection Area for birds: take binoculars. For the history enthusiast there is an ancient laundry, a castle and an interpretation centre devoted to Moorish culture.

Starting from La Parada with the bus stop and restaurant on your left, walk straight up the main street, Calle Casas Nuevas, in the direction of Centro Urbano. At a junction with a big house, No 52, go left to ascend Calle Huertas. At the next junction, which has three options, keep left. Walk straight ahead, ignoring the turning to the right. The lane bends to the right and ascends steeply. At a T-junction go left, and at the following T-junction also go left. Ascend to the top of the village and a T-junction at a small **water station** and go left on the wide, well-made lane laid with cobbles. ▶

Come to a building on the left, which is a restored public **laundry**, La Fuente de los Moros. This point is the start of the Valley of the Moors and the route by which the exiled Moors left Extremadura.

The sierra is ahead and the town behind.

> In 1502 Ferdinand and Isabella signed an expulsion order against the **Moors**. Hornachos became the most populated centre for those who elected to stay in Spain, and by the end of the 16th century there were many thousands living within the walls of the town. On 9 April 1609, Phillip II expelled all the remaining Moors from Spain; they left Hornachos by walking over the sierra and eventually settled in what is now Morocco. With their departure Hornachos declined in wealth and importance.

There are information boards and various route options and waymarks, including a lilac one which this route follows for a while. Continue ahead on the now rocky earth track, which is well-defined, as it ascends and narrows. Reach a small grassy triangle: the track goes ahead, but turn right. There is evidence of a rockfall and just to right of this is a narrow path. Take this path.

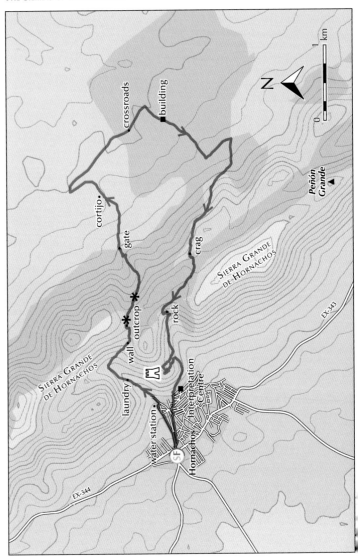

The path is rocky and ascends through head-height cistus bushes. ▸ Reach a clear area with a **wall** ahead; the path bends to the left to follow the wall, now on the right. Come to a T-junction, go left and continue the ascent past mature cork oak trees. Reach a crossroads and continue ahead. Within metres come to a T-junction and bend left to reach a large rocky **outcrop** ahead and right. Continue on the path to walk around the outcrop, keeping it on the right. Once around the outcrop come to a **viewpoint** and enjoy a stunning panorama out towards the east.

Look left for views of the town.

Descend on the narrow rocky path with the view ahead, an outcrop of rock on the left and an extensive view of the ridge of the sierra on the right. Keep on the path all the way down the side of the sierra, passing a small turning on the left that reaches another **viewpoint**.

Near the bottom of the descent there are a few zig-zags but no junctions. Pass through shady oak copses to reach a **gate**. Do not go through but turn right to descend the earth path with a fence on the left. Enter an extensive area of cork oak trees as the path widens to become an almost flat earth track. Pass the gates to

Looking east from the first climb

a large whitewashed **cortijo** on the left, and reach a T-junction with metal gates on the left. Turn right at the small waymark.

Continue on the wide track to a Y-junction and stay right. (There is a yellow waymark for the Ruta de la Umbria.) Pass over a dry stream bed, and just afterwards reach a **crossroads** identified with a yellow waymark on the right. However, do not go right but go straight ahead. At a T-junction, turn right to walk towards the sierra, ignoring other junctions. Pass a white **building** on the right, then go through a set of metal gates. Keep straight ahead and ascend.

Pass a low wall on the left and immediately reach a T-junction. Go left. (There is a yellow waymark, also directing to the left.) Reach a crossroads and turn right onto a grassy track heading for the sierra; it narrows to a soft earth path and ascends through bushes and trees. Ignore a turning to the left and continue on the main path.

Come to where the path goes left, then right, to reach a rocky **crag** and a viewpoint. The ascent continues more steeply to pass through a magical old oak copse with trees covered in fruticose lichen and outcrops of rocks towering overhead on the left.

Reach a stretch of granite-edged earth steps to help the ascent. The path becomes wider, lined with boulders on either side. Ignore a cutting on the left that leads to a path and keep straight on the almost flat path. As it starts to descend there is a view, ahead and left, of the castle.

The path descends, gets rougher, and passes a huge **rock** on the right. The path, made of laid cobbles, zig-zags steeply downwards with views of Hornachos and the castle ahead. Come to a small cutting, right, from which there is a defined footpath up to the castle. Follow the path to a wall and turn left to reach the **castle**. ◀

Take care when exploring as there are no safety measures at all.

Castillo Mora, now only ruins, sits on a commanding hill behind Hornachos. It was originally built by the Berbers in the ninth century to defend the town, which had been a settled area since Roman

Castillo Mora

times. Hornachos had been an important part of the Empire's trading activity because of its productive iron mines.

The return is from the front of the castle, down to the left, between the castle walls and entrance façade, to turn left and then hairpin right to follow the path back to the main walk path. Turn right to continue the walk.

Descend some well-made cobbled steps to reach an open area above the town where there are information boards. Descend to the right and reach the **Interpretation Centre** for Moorish Culture on the right, then descend the slope towards Calle Retiro. Turn right and keep going down. Join Calle Parras at a T-junction, turn left to cross the Plaza de España, and walk left down Calle Hernán Cortés to join Calle Casas Nuevas again. Turn left and reach La Parada once more.

SIERRA MORENA

WALK 29
Cabeza la Vaca and the Sierra de Buitrera

Start/Finish	Calle Tomillar, Cabeza la Vaca
Distance	12km
Ascent/Descent	420m
Time	3hrs
Terrain	Village streets, dirt tracks, earth footpaths
Max altitude	938m
Map	IGN 897 Monesterio 1:50,000
Refreshments	Bars, cafés and restaurants in Cabeza la Vaca
Access	By car: reach Cabeza la Vaca via the EX-103 from Monesterio. Turn right off the EX-103 into the village at the sign. The road leading into the village is Calle Tomillar.
Parking	In Calle Tomillar, just before the entrance to Cabeza la Vaca
Waymarks	Signposts, white and yellow flashes – but not all are for this walk
Spring water	None en route
Note	Some parts of the walk do not have shade

This gentle walk takes in rural countryside typical of the Sierra Morena; rolling pasture, holm and cork oak woods, stream beds with deciduous trees, grazing animals, extensive views and bird activity in the skies above. Almost all the route is on easy dirt tracks with seasonally lush verges.

Walk away from the village, back along Calle Tomillar, passing a garage with a good little cafeteria – San Benito – on the right. (Opposite this is a map and information board of walks in the area.) Reach the junction with the EX-103: just before the junction, on the right, is an open

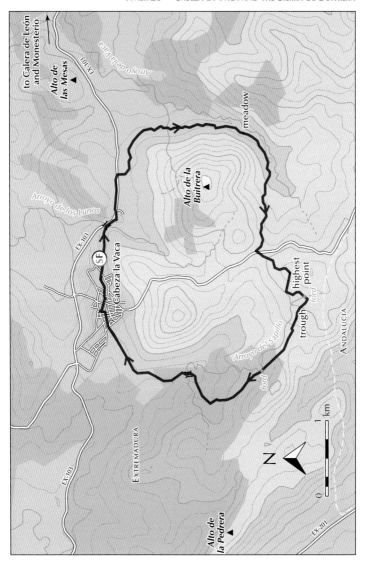

Gentle hills below the Sierra de Buitrera

space. Turn right here to walk over the **bridge** and along the track to join the EX-103, which is on the left.

Cross over the road and take the wide track as it bends right and shadows the road, now on the right. At the end of the track reach the EX-103 once more. There is a signpost for 'Ruta de la Buitrera'. Cross the road, walk left for a few paces and turn right up a waymarked track, and at the top of a short climb reach a T-junction. Turn left.

Follow the dirt track through an area of pasture and oak trees where there may be sheep, goats and pigs. Ignore all junctions to keep on the main track ahead. At a distinctive Y-junction keep right, and at a second Y-junction also keep right. Occasional streams run down from the right to flow left under the track.

Pass through a wooded area of mixed trees. A stream runs on the left and comes close to the track before meandering away through an open **meadow** – a good bird-spotting area. ◄ The track continues to ascend.

Opposite is a view of the Sierra de Buitrera.

GRIFFON VULTURES

Buitre is Spanish for vulture. *Buitre Leonado* refers to the griffon vulture, the most common vulture in Extremadura – although its status in Europe is vulnerable. Griffon vultures are easy to identify; they are big birds with a wingspan of over 2.5m. Their body and wings are brown but their feathers are black. They usually fly in groups of three or more in quite close formation. They are hard to miss and seem to circle most peaks.

Reach a signpost and junction on the right but ignore this turning and walk ahead. Within a few paces reach a tarmac lane and a multi-junction where there are many signposts for optional walks. Cross the lane and walk left for a few paces to reach a dirt track on the right with a waymark and signpost, 'Camino de la Quebrada'. Within metres reach a Y-junction: right is the 'Camino de Cerro Molino', but go left even though there are white and yellow crosses on the left.

The rough track ascends into a shady wooded area with splendid views on the right. Pass finca and small house entrances. The views on the left and behind are extensive. Reach a wide metal gate where the track bends right to run alongside an open meadow on the right, then reach the **highest point** of the walk.

The track descends quite steeply with a stunning view ahead of wooded sierras. At the bottom of the descent, cross a **ford** (stepping-stones). The track becomes narrower and rougher, shaded with trees. Ascend another short climb to reach a T-junction and go right. Pass a granite water **trough** on the right (not drinking water).

Reach a Y-junction. Ignore the right turn – there is a white and yellow cross – and go left to reach a T-junction. Go right, and at a junction with a track on the left, keep on the main track ahead. This descends steeply past a huge chestnut wood on the left with glimpses of the village ahead and right.

Cross a **ford** and reach a T-junction with a well-made dirt lane. Turn right onto the lane, which descends giving a superb view ahead of a wooded sierra slope. A stream

The shady track with the chestnut wood on the left

runs by the lane on the right before reaching a cork oak wood. Cross a **bridge** over the stream.

The lane ascends towards the village, passing the primary school on the right. Walk straight ahead up Calle Muladar and at a crossroads go straight ahead. Take a left down Del Medio to reach the plaza and walk down La Tienda. Reach Plaza Vieja and a fountain in the centre of the street. Go left and ahead along Calle Tomillar to turn left at the end and reach the starting point on the outskirts of **Cabeza la Vaca**.

WALK 30

Monasterio de Tentudía and Pico Tentudía

Start/Finish	Ronda Fuentes de León, Monesterio
Distance	19km
Ascent/Descent	740m
Time	5–6hrs
Terrain	Tarmac roads and lanes, dirt lanes, tracks and footpaths, rocky stream bed
Max altitude	1091m
Map	IGN 897 Monesterio 1:50,000
Refreshments	Monesterio has a good range of bars, cafés and restaurants; there is a café next to the monastery, El Balcón de Tentudía.
Access	By car: Monesterio is signposted in both directions from the E-803 and N-630
Parking	Anywhere on the Ronda Fuentes de León where there are lay-bys
Waymarks	A few hand painted signs, white and yellow flashes
Spring water	None en route
Note	Not much shade on the route within 2.5km of the monastery. Part of the walk is over a stream bed and this may not be possible just after very heavy rain.

This excellent walk goes steadily upwards from Monesterio all the way to the Monastery of Tentudía and the highest point in Badajoz province. It starts through a rural farming landscape with lush flowering verges, some fig and olive fincas and meadows with grazing animals – especially pigs. Monesterio is famous for its jamón. The middle part of the walk passes over a stream bed and continues through shady woods of mixed oak, and the final climb towards the monastery is on a tarmac minor road. The view from the top is worth the climb and there are usually griffon vultures circling overhead on the lookout for food. The return more-or-less retraces steps back to Monesterio.

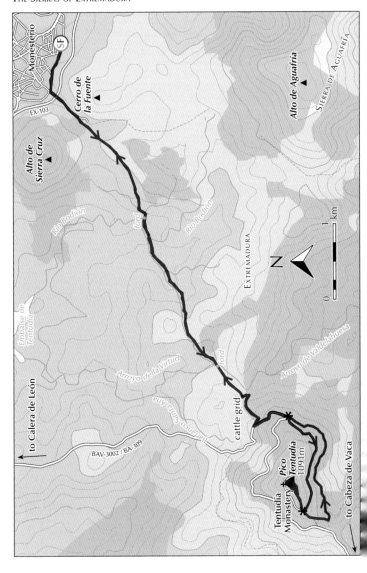

From the Ronda Fuentes de León, walk up the tarmac hill with the town on your right. Descend towards a small crossroads with a tall street light in the centre, and turn left to pass under the **EX-103** through the tunnel.

Walk ahead on the small lane, which becomes compacted earth. Just after a round building and a utility pole, both on the right, take the small track, also right (signed 'Tentudía'). The track bends left to reach a Y-junction. The left track returns to the lane but the right track is signposted 'Ruta de Tentudía'. Follow this track as it goes upwards.

At a Y-junction keep left, and at the next Y-junction keep right as the track descends. ▶ Reach another Y-junction, with 'Tentudía' written on a concrete block gatepost. Keep right and keep descending.

There is a view of Tentudía reservoir on the right.

A small stream, in season, runs along the track. Reach a **ford** with stepping-stones to cross a second water course. The track narrows considerably and runs alongside a small fence on the left with soft rolling hills behind. On the right are lush verges and hedges of flowering bushes.

Outside Monesterio before the climb

The track becomes, in effect, the stream bed and the banks on either side indicate that the stream could be 30–40cm deep in times of prolonged rain. In less wet times there are stepping-stones to negotiate the stream bed. In summer, it is dry. Pass two white and yellow way-marks painted on concrete fence posts, left. Pass, also left, an ancient gateway to Dehesa Arroyo – *arroyo* being the Spanish word for stream.

Still in the stream bed, the path becomes rockier and ascends. Just on the brow of the ascent the rocky stream bed disappears, leaving a soft earth track going through a shady tunnel created by holm oak branches overhead. The track leaves the tunnel to become wider, and runs downwards between two dry stone walls beyond which, on either side, is the *dehesa*.

> The **Extremeño Dehesa** is a distinctive feature of the landscape and can only be described as extensive parkland. The holm oak trees, spaced out within the meadows and pastures, are pruned to encourage the trees to grow outward and not upward. This means that each tree gives maximum shade. Pigs, sheep, goats and cattle graze the dehesa. The holm oaks provide acorns loved by the pigs and the wood is used as fuel for heating.

Reach a **ford** with a stream running from left to right at the bottom of the descent. Cross it using the stepping-stones. The track now ascends gently to join a well-made wider lane coming from the right. Turn left to find a second gateway to Dehesa Arroyo on the left and a **cattle grid** and an unlocked gate (for those who do not like cattle grids) ahead. There is a sign: 'Monte U.P. No1 Tudía y sus Faldas'. Cross the grid and follow the lane as it bends left and ascends.

Reach a Y-junction called Puerto de la Cruces and keep right. There is a farm on the right. Ignore the junction to the farm, as the lane ascends to reach a second cattle grid and gate. Cross over and walk ahead to a stop sign and a T-junction with the BAV-3002/BA-309. Turn

left to follow this tarmac road as it ascends towards the monastery.

Inside Tentudía Monastery

Just as the road makes a zig-zag, reach a lay-by on the left with a plethora of signs and information boards for the area, El Monte Tudía y Sus Faldas ('Tudía Mountain and its skirts' – see Walk 31). There is a lovely **viewpoint**.

The walk to Tentudía monastery continues up the road. Reach a junction on the right going to Cabeza de Vaca. There is a sign for the monastery (2km). Keep ascending, and just as the road bends to the right reach a crossroads and signposts for walk options. Take the rough track on the right and ascend the short distance to the **monastery**, which sits on the highest point in Badajoz province. ▶

This is a good place to rest, explore, enjoy the views and watch the birds.

TENTUDÍA MONASTERY

A legend, from the time of the Reconquest, records that night was falling during a battle between Christians and Moors, fought on the slopes of the Sierra Morena. The conflict was going in the favour of the Christians, but had not yet been won decisively. Pelay Pérez Correa, Captain of the Christian army, cried out to the Virgin Mary to 'Hold the day' or '*Tiend tu día*'. God heard and did just that. The Christians were granted enough daylight to secure the victory. The monastery was built by the Order of St James to mark this historic battle.

The monastery can be visited and the entrance fee is €1 (2017). There is also a café El Balcón de Tentudía where the food is good.

Retrace your steps to the signposts at the crossroads and go straight over. Follow the steep track as it descends to a T-junction with signposts – a good **viewpoint**. Turn left; the track continues to descend but less steeply. Reach a junction with signposts but ignore the turning on the right and keep straight on the track, now ascending. At a second signposted junction, ignore the track that drops sharply to the right. Continue on the main track to reach the El Monte Tudía y Sus Faldas lay-by on the BAV-3002/BA-309 once more. Turn right and retrace your steps back to **Monesterio**.

WALK 31

Forest circuit in the Sierra Tudía y Sus Faldas

Start/Finish	Signposted area at El Monte Tudía y Sus Faldas on the BAV-3002/BA-309
Distance	15km; including detour to visit monastery: 17km
Ascent/Descent	430m; including detour: 570m
Time	4½hrs; including detour: 6hrs
Terrain	Woodland tracks throughout. (One steep rough track to access the monastery.)
Max altitude	974m; including detour: 1091m
Map	IGN 897 Monesterio 1:50,000
Refreshments	There is a good café, El Balcón de Tentudía, next to the monastery
Access	By car: reach the start from Monesterio, via the EX-103, taking the turning to the Monasterio de Tentudía signposted opposite the turning to Calera de León. Follow the BAV-3002/BA-309 to the sign for 'El Monte' on the left, just 2km below the monastery.
Parking	In the signposted parking area at El Monte Tudía y Sus Faldas on the BAV-3002/BA-309
Waymarks	Signposts and waymarks in blue. Ignore all junctions except as signed.
Spring water	None en route
Note	There is shade all the way around except the last 2.5km. On hot days, walk late to get a cool evening finish or do the walk in reverse and start early.

Lovers of trees, quiet, shade and soft woodland tracks will enjoy this walk. There are information boards within the forest about the trees, and there are abundant flowering bushes; white and pink cistus, lavender, broom, Mediterranean Daphne and Spanish heath. Wildflowers bloom in spring, especially by the stream. Songbirds, wood pigeons and woodpeckers can be heard but not necessarily seen. Vultures and kites soar in the skies. On the higher parts of the walk the views are of forested slopes and the Monastery of Tentudía perched on its peak.

After stopping at the **viewpoint**, walk between the gate-posts and descend to reach a junction on the left. Here are multiple signs for walk options: Ruta de Exosistemas Forestales (blue), Ruta de la Pantaneta (Red) and Ruta del Paraje de Moro (white and yellow). Turn left and follow the blue signs.

Reach a junction on the left and turn sharp left to descend lower than the initial track, with uninterrupted views of round forested hills and open pasture unfolding.

Within the **forests** are four types of oak to look out for: *Quercus ilex*, *Quercus rotundifolia*, *Quercus suber* and *Quercus pyrenaica*. The two main types

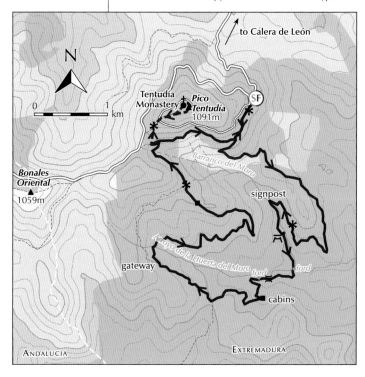

The track by the Arroyo de la Huerta

of pine are *Pinus pinea* and *Pinus pinaster*, a resinous tree with a deep fragrance of its own. There is an area of Spanish chestnut, *Castanea sativa*, towards the end of the walk, and species of alder, *Alnus viridis*, grow along the streams.

The descent continues to come to a staggered crossroads. Turn left, then right as indicated by the waymark. Reach an open area with another crossroads and a fence barring the main track ahead to prevent vehicle access. Go through the fence using the loop over the post on the left and continue ahead through an area of verges lined with bushes and pines.

Ignore a junction with a track going left and back, and keep ahead. Come to a flatter, more open area with a huge pine forest on the right with a meadow in front – flower-filled in the spring. On the left is a cork oak wood.

At a Y-junction follow the track as it makes an acute bend, right. The track narrows and runs through a dense pine forest where birdsong is the only noise apart from footfall. ▸ Pass a metal gate on the left and a small house. Reach a T-junction with four **signposts** for the previous

On the left and ahead is a view of Tentudía Monastery.

205

Tentudía Monastery

In spring the verges are lush and flower-filled with profuse butterflies and bird activity.

walks plus El Pinar. Turn left over a natural bridge (the stream flows under the path) and walk with the Barranco del Moro on the left.

Come to a **picnic area** on the left with tables and benches and two defunct water fountains. There is also a car parking area. Reach a junction, ignore the right turn, and walk ahead to cross the Arroyo de la Huerta del Moro by a ford. Within metres reach a T-junction and turn right. The stream now runs on the right. ◄

Reach a **bridge** over the stream and continue, ascending slightly. Cross a **ford** and come to a junction with five options. Follow the waymark to turn left where the track makes an acute left to go back on itself – but at a higher altitude. On the left reach a series of wooden **cabins**: Cabañas del Tentudía, a holiday area. The track hairpins right.

As the track ascends gradually there are views of the monastery on the right. Reach another junction with five options and multiple waymarks. Turn right to pass an imposing **gateway** to a house, and just afterwards there is a small turning going right and downwards. The track is soft earth and descends and winds through the trees down into the folds of the valley. Cross several fords and pass a fenced olive grove on the right.

A few metres before a T-junction there is a turning, left, that ascends slightly. Take this and pass a large white building – a store for the village of Calera de Leon, which is responsible for the forests. Reach a wooden fenced area on the right with chestnut trees. ▶ Continue on the track, ignoring the junction to the left. The track ascends and is wider with wide verges and therefore not much shade in the middle of the day. By a countryside interpretation board on the right (in Spanish), there is a superb **viewpoint**.

Reach a junction: on the left is an optional ascent to the Monastery of Tentudía.

Detour to the monastery

The signposted track goes up very steeply to reach a crossroads with multiple signposts. Cross straight over and continue the ascent to the monastery on a rough track. See Walk 30 for information about the monastery.

After visiting the area and enjoying the views, descend to meet the junction at the bottom of the hill once more. Turn left to pick up the track and left again to continue as signposted.

Continuing on the main route, all the views are on the right as the track rises and falls along the side of the sierra. Reach the junction, now right, at the start of the circular walk. Continue ahead to arrive back at the parking area.

There is a wonderful view of the monastery ahead.

WALK 32

Alto de Aguafría and the Sierra de Aguafría

Start/Finish	Ronda Fuentes de León, Monesterio
Distance	12.5km
Ascent/Descent	480m
Time	4hrs
Terrain	Compacted earth lane, woodland tracks occasionally concreted on severe ascents/descents, soft earth footpaths
Max altitude	1071m
Map	IGN 897 Monesterio 1:50,000
Refreshments	Monesterio has a good range of bars, cafés and restaurants.
Access	By car: Monesterio is well signposted in both directions from the E-803 and N-630.
Parking	Anywhere on the Ronda Fuentes de León where there are lay-bys
Waymarks	Patchy: white and yellow flashes, fingerposts
Spring water	None en route

Almost all of this walk is within a forest of pine, chestnut and other deciduous trees. There are a few madroño trees with fruit ready to be eaten by November. In open spaces there are low-growing flowering shrubs, especially pink cistus and vibernium, but in the spring tall asphodels carpet the forest floor. While birds of prey circle above, smaller birds fill the woods with their song. From the neglected 'castle' there are very fine views.

Directly ahead on the sierra is a fire watchtower, the highest point of the walk.

From the Ronda Fuentes de León, walk up the tarmac hill with the town on your right. Descend towards a small crossroads with a tall street light in the centre, and turn left to pass under the EX-103 through the **tunnel**.

Walk ahead on the small lane, which becomes compacted earth. ◄ Pass a sign on the left for 'Sierra de Aguafría', which simply signposts the area. Reach

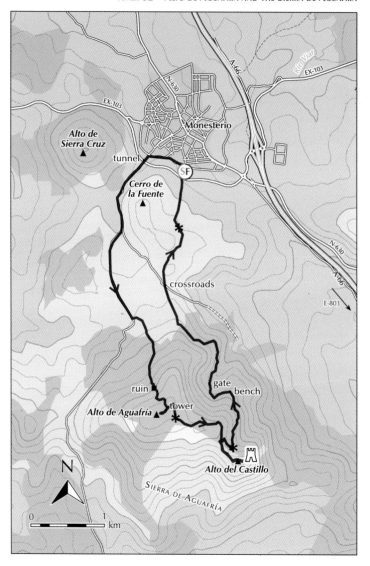

a turning to the left with a sign, 'Ruta del Castillo' and an information board; do not turn left here but continue on the lane past meadows and small agricultural buildings. Come to a turning, left, with signs for the 'Sierra de Aguafría, Ruta de Aguafría, Castillo' and information boards. Take this turning, left.

The track passes a few agricultural buildings and small fincas. It ascends as it enters a wood of chestnut, deciduous oak and pine. Ignore all junctions and keep on the wide track as it ascends relentlessly through the wood – the track bends but there is no possibility of getting lost as it is very clear. Pass a few shady eucalyptus trees and reach a large pile of rocks on the left as the track bends left. Just afterwards, also on the left, reach a building, now a **ruin**, covered in vegetation.

At the top of the long climb reach a new track cutting left to right across the track. Turn very slightly right, then left, to continue on the track as it goes straight up. At the top of the climb reach a Y-junction: turn right to follow the well-made dirt track to the **watchtower** and the highest point of the walk, Alto de Aguafría. (Unfortunately the views are restricted by the trees.)

Retrace your steps to the Y-junction and go straight on, ignoring the left turn which was the way up. ◄ Ignore small turnings left and right, and keep on the well-made track as it bends right and left and ascends and descends.

To the left through the trees are views of hill after hill after hill stretching into the distance.

Come to a Y-junction. Do not go right, but continue down the track and come to a fine **view** of Monesterio on the left. Descend steeply, and at an acute turning to the left, look right. There is a small track with signposts: take this track and follow it through an open area of low-growing bushes to reach a T-junction. Go left to reach another open area with a huge outcrop of granite ahead and right. The track ascends, and bends left to come to a reconstructed stretch of granite paving indicative of how the track may have been in the past. Reach the **castle**.

Alto del Castillo is really only a small reconstructed tower, now neglected. The surrounding area provides extensive views. At the time of writing (2017) the handrails to the steps going up to the top of the tower were unsafe. Take care.

Retrace your steps back to the T-junction and turn right. Reach the original woodland track and turn right again. Follow the track as it descends in hairpin bends to reach a sharp left bend with a superb **view** of the sierra side and the far hills on the right. Ignore tracks to the left and right as the track bends left.

Just here is a small bench on the left and an **inscription**, 'These beautiful mountain landscapes are the legacy of our ancestors. With hard work and dedication we have cared for them throughout our lives for the use and enjoyment of future generations.' The two brothers, both named on the inscription, lived to be over 80, so they must have done something right!

The track descends into chestnut trees mixed with pines. Pass a water tank on the left and reach a few houses on the right and one on the left. Come to a locked

View to the south from Alto del Castillo

211

The single-file footpath back towards Monesterio

metal **gate** to deter vehicles but there is gap for walkers on the right. Reach a Y-junction but stay on the track to go up and left. Reach a T-junction: there is a house on the right and another, 'El Robledillo', ahead. A woodland path goes up on the left but the return to Monesterio is the track on the right just past the house on the right.

Follow the descending track through an agricultural landscape. At a **crossroads** go straight over. The track narrows to become a single-file footpath and on a left bend there is a good **view** of Monesterio. Bear right to join a track and start a very steep descent to the EX-103 on a concreted stretch of the track. Cross straight over the EX-103 and descend to arrive at the by-pass and a signpost, 'Aguafrías Castillo Fin de Ruta'.

APPENDIX A

Route summary table

Walk no	Name	Distance	Time	Max altitude	Total ascent/ descent	Page
Northern sierras						
1	San Martín de Trevejo and the Sierra de Eljas	19km	6hrs	1058m	710m	33
2	Pico Jálama	9km	3hrs	1487m	540m	41
3	Puerto de Castilla and Pico Jañona	16km	6hrs	1353m	800m	46
4	Castillo de Almenara and the Sierra de las Jañonas	10km	3hrs	997m	450m	52
5	Robledillo de Gata and Ovejuela	16km	6hrs	1008m	960m	57
6	La Garganta and El Nevero	7km	2hrs	1268m	220m	62
7	La Muela and the forest track	14.5km	5hrs	1605m	640m	66
8	Valley route to La Muela	15.5km	4½hrs	1605m	700m	71
9	Cascadas Nogaleas in the Montes de Tras la Sierra	7km	3hrs	810m	470m	76
10	Los Pilones and Puente Sacristán	12km	4½hrs	832m	500m	81
11	Jerte to Puente Nuevo in the Sierra de Tormantos	16km	5½hrs	958m	570m	85
12	Puente los Papúos in the Montes de Tras de Sierra	6km	1½hrs	836m	270m	91
13	The Jaranda valley	14km	5hrs	915m	656m	94
14	Guijo de Santa Bárbara and El Trabuquete	11.5km	6hrs	1475m	840m	100
Central sierras						
15	Arroyomolinos	13km	5hrs	870m	570m	107
16	Torre de Santa María to Montánchez	13km	4hrs	740m	400m	113

Walk no	Name	Distance	Time	Max altitude	Total ascent/ descent	Page
17	Torre de Santa María and the mills	10.5km	3½hrs	775m	320m	119
18	The oak woods of Zarza de Montánchez	13km	4hrs	725m	350m	125
19	Almoharín and the Sierra de San Cristobal	13.5km	5hrs	825m	590m	130
20	The Sierra de los Alijares	7.5km	3hrs	738m	300m	137
21	The Sierra de Santa Cruz	8.5km	5hrs	808m	420m	142
22	Garganta de Cuernacabras	13km	5hrs	648m	490m	148
23	Garciaz and Pico Venero	17.5km	5½hrs	1128m	630m	153
24	Cabañas del Castillo to Navezuelas	12.5km	4hrs	1042m	720m/560m	160
25	Navezuelas to Guadalupe	15km	5hrs	1230m	650m/910m	166
26	Orellana de la Sierra	7.5km	2½hrs	635m	340m	173
Southern sierras						
27	La Zarza	17.5km or 7.5km	5hrs or 2½hrs	500m	550m or 340m	179
28	Hornachos	14km	5hrs	778m	670m	186
29	Cabeza la Vaca and the Sierra de Buitrera	12km	3hrs	938m	420m	192
30	Monasterio de Tentudía and Pico Tentudía	19km	5–6hrs	1091m	740m	197
31	Forest circuit in the Sierra de Tudía y Sus Faldas	15km or 17km	4½hrs or 6hrs	974m or 1091m	430m or 570m	203
32	Alto de Aguafría and the Sierra de Aguafría	12.5km	4hrs	1071m	480m	208

APPENDIX B

Link route summary table

Walk numbers	Walk name	Distance	Time	Max altitude	Total ascent/ descent
6 & 7	El Nevero, La Muela and the forest track	20km	6½hrs	1605m	750m
6 & 8	El Nevero, the valley route and La Muela	21km	6½hrs	1605m	790m
6, 7 & 8	El Nevero, the valley route, La Muela and the forest track	24km	7½hrs	1605m	830m
7 & 8	The valley route, La Muela and the forest track	18.5km	6hrs	1605m	760m
10 & 11	Los Pilones and Puente Nuevo	16.5km	5hrs	958m	650m
13 & 14	The Jaranda valley, Guijo de Santa Bárbara and El Trabuquete	26km	8hrs	1475m	1400m
18 & 19	Zarza de Montánchez and Almoharín	26km	8hrs	825m	930m
24 & 25	Cabañas del Castillo, Navezuelas and Guadalupe	28km	9hrs	1230m	1370m/ 1470m

APPENDIX C
Additional waymarked routes in the area

Sierra de Gata
The GR10-E7 crosses the Sierra de Gata from the border with Las Hurdes to that of Portugal. It runs through Robledillo de Gata, Descargamaría, Cadalso, Gata, Torre de San Miguel, Villabuenas de Gata, Perlas del Puerto, Hoyos, Acebo, San Martín de Trevejo, Villamiel, Trevejo and Cilleros. The route is waymarked in red and white with named posts at intervals.

Sierra de Béjar
PR CC-37, 'Los Bosques del Ambroz', starts in La Garganta. The first stage of this famous walk goes to Hervás, 10km. The middle stage goes to Gargantilla, 17.5km in total. The final part goes to Segura de Toro, 22km in total. All one-way, waymarked in white and yellow.

Sierra de Gredos
PR CC-1, 'Ruta Carlos V', starts in Tornavacas, takes in Puente Nuevo from Walk 11, and finishes in Jarandilla de la Vera. It is 26km. Waymarked with signposts and in white and yellow.

PR CC-2, 'Ruta del Cerezo en Flor', also starts in Tornavacas but incorporates Jerte. It is 22.5km long and is best enjoyed during cherry blossom time in the spring. Waymarked with signposts and in white and yellow.

PR CC-14, 'Ruta Garganta de los Infiernos', starts and finishes in Jerte and is 16km. Waymarked with signposts and in white and yellow, but the way down from the Puente del Carrascal is hard to find.

Sierra de Montánchez
PR CC-28, 'Ruta de las Vaquerizas', PR CC-29, 'Ruta del Robledo' and PR CC-30, 'Ruta de las Aguas', are all local routes near Montánchez. The signposting is vague in places, however no one will get completely lost.

'Ruta de Sierra de San Cristobal' starts and finishes in Almoharin and is 18km. Signposted throughout.

'Ruta del Risco Grande' starts and finishes in Santa Cruz de la Sierra and is 8km out-and-back.

SL CC-253, 'Sierra del Puerto', also starts and finishes in Santa Cruz de la Sierra. 5.45km out-and-back.

Sierra de Guadalupe
Guadalupe has been a centre for pilgrimage since 1326. All the routes, except for the first, end in Guadalupe. The distance is one-way.

GR 116, 'Camino Natural de las Villuercas', runs from Logrosán, detours into Guadalupe, and ends in Rincon del Torozo in Castilla la Mancha. It is 76.5km.

GR 117, 'Alfonso Onceno', starts in Avellaneda and is 59km. Walk 25 is the last stage of this route.

GR 118, 'Camino de los Jerónimos', starts at Yuste Monastery in the Sierra de Gredos and is 56.7km. This route unites the two Hieronymite monasteries.

GR 119, 'Camino Real de Guadalupe', starts in Puente del Arzobispo and is 62.9km.

GR 212, 'Camino de los Montes de Toledo'. This route starts in Toledo. It is 196km. All are waymarked in white and red with helpful signposts at intervals.

Sierra Morena

'Ruta del Pantaneta' starts and finishes in the signposted area at El Monte Tudía y Sus Faldas on the BAV-3002/BA-309. The route is 7.1km. Waymarked in red.

PR-BA, 'Ruta del Paraje del Moro', starts and finishes at the Tentudía Monastery, and is 11.7km. Waymarked in white and yellow.

APPENDIX D

Useful contacts

Transport

Air

British Airways
www.britishairways.com

Easyjet
www.easyjet.com

Ryanair
www.ryanair.com

Vueling
www.vueling.com

Norwegian
www.norwegian.com

Lufthansa
www.lufthansa.com

KLM
www.klm.com

Tap Portugal
www.flytap.com

Rail

Spanish national rail network
www.renfe.com
(English-language option available)

Bus

From Portugal

www.avanzabus.com
(English-language option available)

Northern sierras

www.nortedeextremadura.es/servicios_de_transporte.aspx (Spanish)

www.mirat-transportes.es
(Spanish; select 'Horarios')

Central sierras

www.solistour.com
(Spanish; select 'Horario Autobuses')

www.venta.avanzabus.com
(English-language option available)

www.unionbusextremadura.com
(Spanish; select 'Información', then
'Rutas y horarios')

Southern sierras

www.leda.es

www.alsa.es

Car hire

www.car-hire-international.com

www.avis.com

www.budget.com

www.enterprise.com

www.europcar.com

www.hertz.co.uk

www.nationalcar.co.uk

Ferry

www.brittany-ferries.co.uk

Weather

www.eltiempo.es

Tourist offices
This site, run by the Junta de
Extremadura Department of Tourism, is
excellent and kept up-to-date. Click on
the language button to get English.
www.turismoextremadura.com

Northern sierras

Baños de Montemayor

Avenida de la Temas, 41
10750 Baños de Montemayor
Cáceres
tel (0034) 927 488 285
www.banosdemontemayor.es

Hervás

Calle Braulio Navas, 6
10700 Hervás
Cáceres
tel (0034) 927 473 618
www.turismodehervas.com

Jarandilla de la Vera

Plaza de la Constitución, 1
10450 Jarandilla de la Vera
Cáceres
tel (0034) 927 560 460
www.jarandilla.com

Jerte

Paraje de Peñas Albas, s/n
10610 Cabezuela del Valle Cáceres
tel (0034) 927 472 558
www.turismovalledeljerte.com

Robledillo de Gata

Plaza del Vadillo, 1
10867 Robledillo de Gata
Cáceres
tel (0034) 927 671 011
www.sierradegata.es

Central sierras

Cáceres

Plaza Mayor, s/n
10003 Cáceres
tel (0034) 927 111 222
www.turismo.ayto-caceres.es

Guadalupe

Plaza de Santa María de Guadalupe, s/n
10140 Guadalupe
Cáceres
tel (0034) 927 154 128
oficinadeturismoguadalupe.blogspot.
com.es

Trujillo

Plaza Mayor, s/n
10200 Trujillo
Cáceres
tel (0034) 927 322 677
www.turismotrujillo.com

Southern sierras

Alange

Calle Trinidad
06840 Alange
Badajoz
tel (0034) 924 365 219
www.alange.es

Badajoz

Pasaje de San Juan, s/n
06002 Badajoz
tel (0034) 924 224 981
www.turismobadajoz.es

Hornachos

Calle Felipe Trigo, 1
06228 Hornachos
Badajoz
tel (0034) 924 533 533
www.hornachos.es

Mérida

Paseo José Álvarez Saenz de Buruaga,
s/n
06800 Mérida
tel (0034) 924 330 722
www.turismomerida.org

Monesterio

Paseo de Extremadura, 314
06260 Monesterio
tel (0034) 924 516 737
www.monesterio.es

Accommodation
www.walkingextremadura.com/where-
to-stay.html

Maps
Centro Nacional de Información
Geográfica (IGN)
General Ibánez de Ibero 3
28010 Madrid
www.cnig.es

Gisiberica
Aveneda Hernán Cortés, 3
Local bajo, derecha
10001 Cáceres
tel (0034) 927 212 207

Stanfords
12–14 Long Acre
London WC1
www.stanfords.co.uk

APPENDIX E
Glossary

Spanish	English
agua	water
agua potable	drinking water
alcornoque	cork oak
arroyo	stream or ditch
balsa	pool or lake
buitre	vulture
cairn	small pile of rocks
calle	street
camino	lane
campo	country
cañada	wide sheep moving trail
casa rural	rural hotel or guest house
cascada	waterfall
castillo	castle
cerro	hill
chozo	traditional round hut, often thatched
collado	hill
cordel	small sheep moving trail
cordillera	mountain range
carretera/ctra	main road
dehesa	pasture dotted with holm oaks
embalse	reservoir
encina	holm oak
ermita	hermitage
finca	farm, house or land in the country
fuente	fountain, spring

Spanish	English
geodesic	relating to measuring between geographic points
hospedería	a chain of hotels
humilladero	shrine, small chapel near village
mirador	viewpoint
molino	mill
monte	mountain
nevero	cool
pantano	large pond, reservoir
parador	chain of hotels set in historical buildings
peligro, peligroso	danger, dangerous
pinturas repuestres	cave paintings
pozo	well
presa	dam
prohibido	prohibited
puente	bridge
puerto	mountain pass
refugio	refuge, especially in mountains
río	river
risco	crag
roble	deciduous oak
ruta	route
sierra	range of mountains
SL-BA routes	routes in Badajoz province
SL-CC routes	routes in Cáceres province
trashumancia	practice of moving sheep between winter and summer pasture
vado	ford
valle	valley

The path to the pool (Walk 6)

DOWNLOAD THE ROUTE
IN GPX FORMAT

All the routes in this guide are available for download from:

www.cicerone.co.uk/848/GPX

as GPX files. You should be able to load them into most formats of mobile device, whether GPS or smartphone.

When you go to this link, you will be asked for your email address and where you purchased the guide, and have the option to subscribe to the Cicerone e-newsletter.

www.cicerone.co.uk

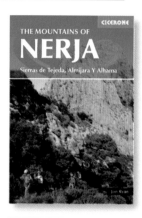
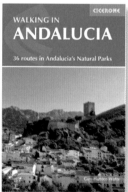
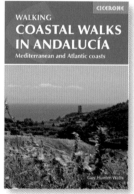

Walking – Trekking – Mountaineering – Climbing – Cycling

Over 40 years, Cicerone have built up an outstanding collection of over 300 guides, inspiring all sorts of amazing adventures.

 Every guide comes from extensive exploration and research by our expert authors, all with a passion for their subjects. They are frequently praised, endorsed and used by clubs, instructors and outdoor organisations.

All our titles can now be bought as **e-books**, **ePubs** and **Kindle** files and we also have an online magazine – **Cicerone Extra** – with features to help cyclists, climbers, walkers and trekkers choose their next adventure, at home or abroad.

Our website shows any **new information** we've had in since a book was published. Please do let us know if you find anything has changed, so that we can publish the latest details. On our **website** you'll also find great ideas and lots of detailed information about what's inside every guide and you can buy **individual routes** from many of them online.

It's easy to keep in touch with what's going on at Cicerone by getting our monthly **free e-newsletter**, which is full of offers, competitions, up-to-date information and topical articles. You can subscribe on our home page and also follow us on **Facebook** and **Twitter** or dip into our **blog**.

Cicerone – the very best guides for exploring the world.

CICERONE

Juniper House, Murley Moss, Oxenholme Road, Kendal, Cumbria LA9 7RL
Tel: 015395 62069 info@cicerone.co.uk
www.cicerone.co.uk and **www.cicerone-extra.com**